Jerry Snyder's
GUITAR SCHOOL

Method Book **1**

This book is designed for you to study material from *both sections* of the book *simultaneously.* You may begin in either **SECTION ONE:** *Chords and Accompaniment* or in **SECTION TWO:** *Learning to Read Music.*

D1535657

Contents

Cover photos: Classical guitar by Richard Bruné;
Martin D-28 courtesy of the Martin Guitar Company;
Fender Stratocaster courtesy of Fender Musical Instruments, Inc.

Alfred

Copyright © MCMXCIII by Alfred Publishing Co., Inc.
All rights reserved. Printed in USA.
ISBN 0-88284-901-8 (Book)   ISBN 0-88284-902-6 (Book and CD)   ISBN 0-7390-0815-3 (CD)

TYPES OF GUITARS

You can learn to play the guitar using any one of several types of guitar: steel string acoustic, nylon string classical, solid body electric, or a semi-hollow body electric. The important thing is that the guitar be properly adjusted for ease of playing. The most critical adjustment is the so-called "action." Action refers to the height of the strings above the fingerboard. If the action is too high, the guitar will be difficult to play. The gauge of the strings on the guitar also contributes to the ease of playing. Gauge is the diameter of a string measured in thousandths of an inch. For example, the first string can vary in string gauge from .008 (light) to .014 (heavy). A guitar with high action and heavy strings will discourage even the most enthusiastic beginner. Make certain that in the beginning, your acoustic or electric steel string guitar has light gauge strings on it, and if you are playing a nylon-string classical, I would recommend light, normal or medium tension strings.

The selection of a guitar is a matter of personal preference. The primary difference between the various guitars is tone quality. Competitive prices have brought both acoustic and electric guitars into the range for the beginner.

Unamplified Acoustic Guitars

STEEL-STRING GUITAR

Manufacturers also describe this guitar as a flat-top guitar or a folk guitar. The body of the guitar is hollow with a flat top, a round soundhole, a pin type bridge, and a pick guard. The neck is fairly narrow and normally joins the body at the 14th fret. The tone quality is bright, brassy, and forceful, and lends itself perfectly to folk, country, ragtime, blues, and pop styles. Beginners should put light gauge strings on their steel string guitar for ease in playing. Bronze strings with ball ends are recommended. The guitar can be played with a pick, with the fingers, or with the thumb and finger picks, fig. 1.

NYLON-STRING CLASSICAL GUITAR

Referred to as the nylon string guitar, classical guitar or folk guitar, this guitar is strung with nylon strings. This contributes to the ease of playing it. The body is hollow with a flat top, and has a round soundhole and a stationary loop type bridge. The neck is wider than that of a steel string guitar. One of the distinguishing characteristics of this guitar is its open peghead. The tone quality might be described as dark, mellow and delicate. This guitar has a rich repertoire of classical music but is also suited for pop, folk, Latin, and jazz. The nylon string guitar is best suited for fingerstyle playing; that is, the strings are plucked with the fingers of the right hand. Never put steel strings on a nylon-string guitar, fig. 2.

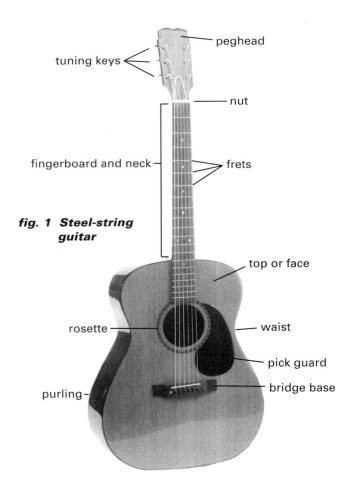

fig. 1 Steel-string guitar

peghead
tuning keys
nut
fingerboard and neck
frets
top or face
rosette
waist
pick guard
purling
bridge base

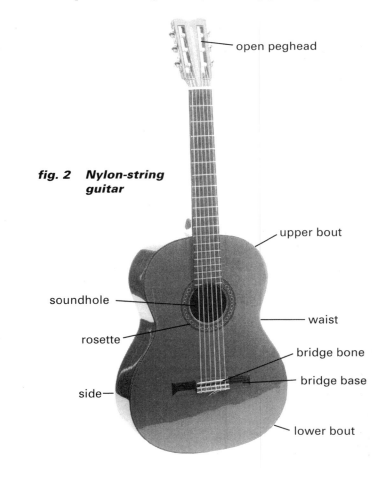

fig. 2 Nylon-string guitar

open peghead
upper bout
soundhole
waist
rosette
bridge bone
side
bridge base
lower bout

ACOUSTIC/ELECTRIC GUITARS

Acoustic steel and nylon string guitars have also gone electric. The phrase acoustic/electric guitar is the best description for what is now possible with the use of various magnetic, contact and transducer type pick-ups which amplify the sound. Some of these pick-ups can be attached to the guitar and some are actually built into the guitar.

Electric Guitars

SOLID BODY ELECTRIC GUITAR

Without amplification, this guitar is too soft to be heard except for individual practice. It relies almost entirely upon the pick-ups and amplifier. The body is solid and comes in a variety of shapes and designs. It has a thin neck and a "cut-away" design to enable the player to play in high positions. In regards to tone quality, there is an emphasis on the trebles (highs); however, a wide variety of tone qualities are possible. There is sustaining power due to the solid body, which absorbs less energy from the string than does an acoustic or semi-acoustic guitar. This is a favorite guitar with blues and rock guitarists, fig. 1.

SEMI-HOLLOW BODY ELECTRIC GUITAR

The body of this guitar is thin and semi-hollow. It has an arched top and back, F-holes and a pick guard. The neck is thin and is attached to the body at the 18th fret. This guitar has a wide range of tone qualities ranging from a fairly dark and mellow sound to the more treble sound of the solid body electric. Without an amplifier, this guitar can barely be heard. The semi-hollow body lends itself to country, rock, jazz, pop and blues styles. It has good sustain and can be played at high volumes without feedback problems, fig. 2.

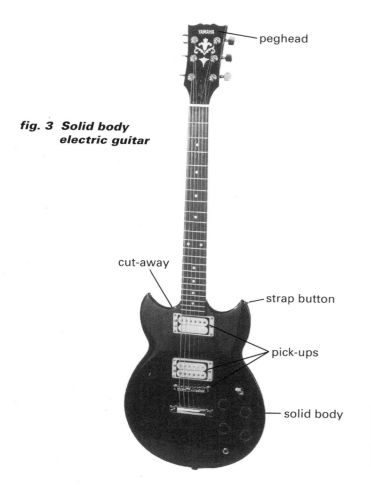

fig. 3 Solid body electric guitar

peghead
cut-away
strap button
pick-ups
solid body

fig. 4 Semi-hollow body electric guitar

tuning machines (tuning keys)
cut-away
upper bout
front pick-up
back pick-up
toggle switch
f-hole
bridge
volume controls
tone controls
arched top

Amplification

A small practice amplifier will be necessary if you begin on an electric guitar. For home practice, a 10 watt amplifier with a 10 inch speaker will be more than adequate. Manufacturers have even smaller practice amps available that may suit your needs. Recently, several companies have developed earphones that can be plugged directly into your guitar. The earphones run on a nine-volt battery and are the cheapest way to hear your guitar.

HOLDING THE GUITAR

Playing positions vary somewhat with the type of guitar, style of music performed, and the right-hand technique being used. There are, however, some basic similarities that are important to observe if you are to develop a good left- and right-hand technique. Study each of the following descriptions.

Sitting Position

Place the waist of the guitar on the right thigh. Tilt the guitar slightly toward you. Keep the neck of the guitar at a 15 degree angle to the floor. Rest the forearm on the edge of the guitar at a point just above the bridge base. Bring the left hand up to the neck of the guitar. The wrist should be kept straight except when playing chords. When you play chords, arch the wrist slightly toward the floor. Never rest the left forearm on your knee or leg, fig. 1.

fig. 1   **Sitting position**

Classical Position

A footstool, fig. 2, is used in the classical position to elevate the left knee to a point where it is higher than the hip. Sit forward in your chair and keep the spine straight. Slumping requires more energy than sitting straight. Pull the right leg back under the chair and balance yourself on the ball of your foot. Place the guitar on the left thigh. The guitar will also touch the inside right thigh, the chest, and the right forearm, fig. 3 and 4.

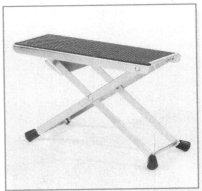

fig. 2   **Footstool**

fig. 3   **Classical position**

Standing Position

A strap is used to hold the guitar when you are standing. Some guitarists even prefer to use a strap when they are sitting. Acoustic guitar straps are generally attached to a pin on the end of the guitar and the head of the guitar just above the nut, fig. 5. Electric guitars usually have a strap button mounted on the body of the guitar plus the end pin, fig. 6.

fig. 5   Standing position

fig. 6   Standing position

fig. 4   Classical position

TUNING THE GUITAR 🔘 Track 1

Learning to tune a guitar is difficult in the beginning. It is an ear training process that will improve with experience. You are training the ear to match one pitch to another. You are learning to determine whether a string on your guitar is the same, higher or lower than a reference or tuning pitch. The tuning pitch is the pitch or tone you are attempting to match. It can be provided by a tuning fork (E), a piano, another guitar, a record or by the guitar itself.

TUNING TECHNIQUE

Listen to the tuning pitch. Determine whether the string you are tuning is the same, higher or lower than the tuning pitch. If guitar sounds lower, you must tighten the string to raise the pitch. If the guitar sounds higher, loosen the string to lower the pitch. If you are not sure if the string is higher or lower, purposely tune the string lower. It is generally easier to approach the tuning pitch from a lower sound pitch than it is to tune down to a pitch. With your left hand gripping the appropriate tuning key, pluck the string with a pick or the thumb as you slowly turn the tuning key. This enables you to hear the pitch change as you are making adjustments to it. Listen to the tuning pitch again. Repeat this procedure until you are satisfied that you have been able to match the tuning pitch.

Tuning to a Piano

Guitar notation sounds an octave (8 notes) lower than written. So when you tune your guitar to a piano, you must be certain that you are tuning the strings to the correct pitch, fig. 6. Play the tuning pitch on the piano and then attempt to match the open guitar string to it. Begin with the 6th string.

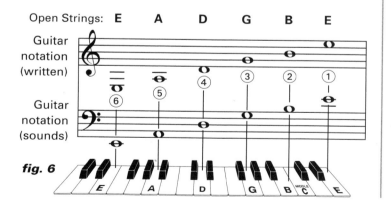

fig. 6

Tuning the Guitar to Itself

The guitar can provide its own tuning pitch. Begin with the 6th string. Either tune it to a tuning pitch provided by some outside source (tuning fork, pitchpipe, piano, record) or estimate the pitch. The pitch of the low E, 6th string usually doesn't vary too much between tunings. Now proceed through the various steps described in fig. 1–5.

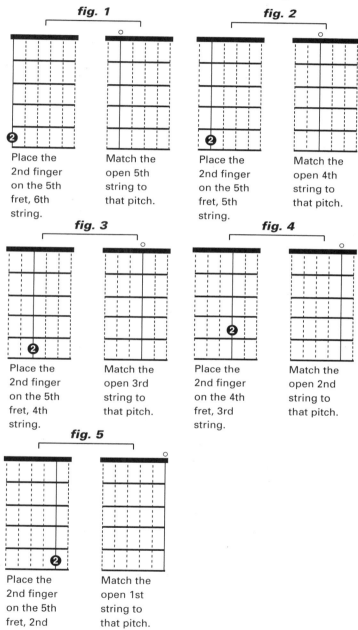

fig. 1 — Place the 2nd finger on the 5th fret, 6th string. Match the open 5th string to that pitch.

fig. 2 — Place the 2nd finger on the 5th fret, 5th string. Match the open 4th string to that pitch.

fig. 3 — Place the 2nd finger on the 5th fret, 4th string. Match the open 3rd string to that pitch.

fig. 4 — Place the 2nd finger on the 4th fret, 3rd string. Match the open 2nd string to that pitch.

fig. 5 — Place the 2nd finger on the 5th fret, 2nd string. Match the open 1st string to that pitch.

Electronic Tuners

There are many inexpensive electronic guitar tuners available that will eliminate the tuning problem for you. They have built-in microphones for acoustic guitars and a chord input for electric guitars. They are well worth the investment.

MUSIC FUNDAMENTALS

Notes and Rests

In music notation, **NOTES** and **RESTS** are the basic symbols used to indicate rhythm. Rhythm refers to the duration, length, or time value given to a note or rest. A **QUARTER NOTE** and **REST** generally represents the basic beat or pulse in music.

fig. 1 Quarter note and rest

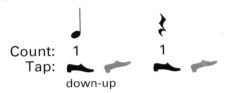

> **QUARTER NOTES** and **RESTS** receive one count or beat. Use your foot to *tap* the rhythm of the quarter note or rest. Each note or rest receives a *down-up* tapping pattern.

fig. 2 Half notes and rest

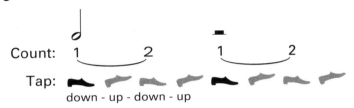

> **HALF NOTES** and **RESTS** receive two counts or beats. Use your foot to *tap* the rhythm of the half note or rest. Each note or rest receives a *down-up-down-up* tapping pattern.

fig. 3 Whole note and rest

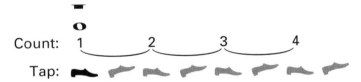

> **WHOLE NOTES** and **RESTS** receive four counts or beats. Use your foot to *tap* the rhythm of the whole note or rest. Each note or rest receives four *down-ups.*

SLASHES are used in guitar notation for repeating rhythm patterns. The abbreviated *slash* notation is often used to notate rhythm guitar parts.

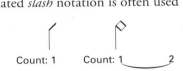

Bar Lines, Measures and Time Signatures

BAR LINES are used to organize notes into **MEASURES** that have the same number of *beats* in them. The most common placement of bar lines is every four beats. **DOUBLE BAR LINES** are used at the end of a song.

The $\frac{4}{4}$ **TIME SIGNATURE** is the most common *time signature.* The top number indicates how many beats are in a

measure. The bottom number tells you what kind of a note receives one beat. The time signature is placed at the beginning of the music.

> **4** = Four beats in each measure
> **4** = A quarter note receives one beat

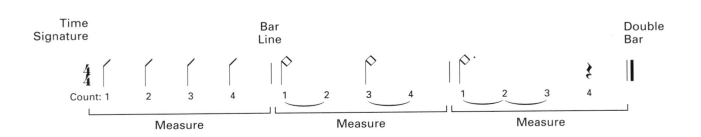

Staff

Notes are placed on a **STAFF** to indicate their *pitch* or *sound.* Pitch refers to the relative high or lowness of a sound. The *staff* has five lines and four spaces, fig. 1. Notes can be placed on a line or in a space, fig. 2 and 3. The higher the note is placed on the staff, the higher the note sounds.

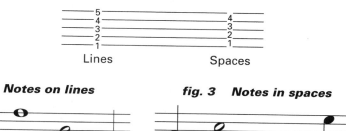

fig. 1   Staff

Lines   Spaces

fig. 2   Notes on lines   **fig. 3   Notes in spaces**

Clef Sign

A **CLEF SIGN** is added to the music staff to indicate what the notes on the lines and spaces represent. Guitar notation uses a **TREBLE** or **G CLEF,** fig. 4. The first seven letters of the alphabet are used to give names to the notes—A, B, C, D, E, F, G. The names of the lines are E, G, B, D, F— **E**very **G**ood **B**oy **D**oes **F**ine. The names of the spaces are F, A, C, E, which spells **FACE.**

fig. 4 The treble clef and names of lines and spaces

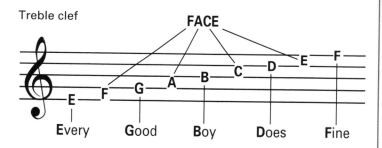

Treble clef

FACE

E   F   G   A   B   C   D   E   F

Every   **G**ood   **B**oy   **D**oes   **F**ine

Frames

FRAMES are used by guitarists to indicate the placement of the *left-hand fingers* on the fingerboard. The *frame* represents the strings and frets of the guitar fingerboard, fig. 5. Numbers placed on or above the frame represent the fingers of the left hand. The letter O stands for an open string and an X or dotted line means not to play the string.

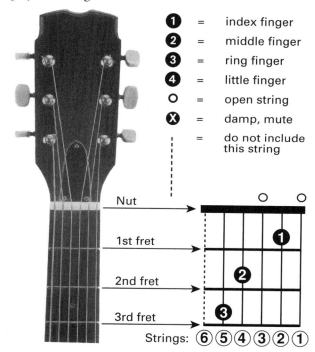

❶	=	index finger
❷	=	middle finger
❸	=	ring finger
❹	=	little finger
O	=	open string
Ⓧ	=	damp, mute
┊	=	do not include this string

Nut

1st fret

2nd fret

3rd fret

Strings: ⑥⑤④③②①

fig. 5 Guitar frame

Tablature

TABLATURE is a six-line staff that graphically represents the guitar fingerboard. Numbers placed on the tablature represent the frets of the guitar. The *fret* and *string* of any note can be indicated by placing a number on the appropriate line of the tablature. Tablature is a system of notation often used in rock, country, folk and blues styles of guitar playing, fig. 6.

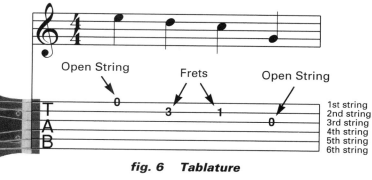

Open String   Frets   Open String

1st string
2nd string
3rd string
4th string
5th string
6th string

fig. 6   Tablature

SECTION ONE
Chords and Accompaniment

This method can be used to learn *either* or *both* **PICKSTYLE** and **FINGERSTYLE** guitar technique. Many of today's guitarists play both styles. Section One begins with chord playing techniques.

Pickstyle

A pick, also called a flat-pick or plectrum, is used to strum the strings of the guitar. Picks come in various sizes, shapes and thicknesses, and are made out of many different kinds of material including plastic, nylon, tortoise shell, rubber, felt and stone. Manufacturers describe the *gauge* or thickness of their picks as light, medium and heavy. I recommend that you use a medium size and thickness pear shape or drop shape pick, fig. 1 and 2.

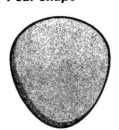

fig. 1
Pear shape

fig. 2
Drop shape

Hold the pick between the thumb and index finger. The pick rests on the top or tip joint of the index finger. Place the thumb over the pick. Press lightly but firmly. The thumb should be kept rigid, fig. 3.

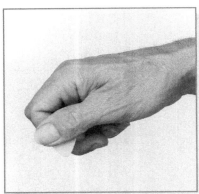

fig. 3   **Holding the pick**

Rest the forearm on the edge of the guitar just above the bridge base, fig. 4.

fig. 4   **Forearm position**

Strum the strings with a pick held between your thumb and index finger. Use a *down-stroke* (⊓) as you strum from the 3rd string downward toward the 1st string, fig. 5 and 6. In the down-stroke, the thumb *pushes* the pick through the strings. When you have completed the strum, return your hand to the starting position.

fig. 5   **Pickstyle preparation**

fig. 6   **Completion**

Fingerstyle

There are a variety of fingerstyle strum techniques. The most basic and perhaps the easiest to learn is the index **finger strum.** I recommend that you avoid strumming with the thumb since it often leads to the development of bad right-hand playing positions. Place the forearm on the edge of the guitar just above the bridge base.

Strum *down* across the strings with the nail of the index finger. The motion of the strum is primarily a finger motion, fig. 1 and 2. This type of strum is often called a **brush, scratch,** or a **finger strum.** Some guitarists prefer to use the index finger and the middle finger when strumming down across the strings.

fig. 1   Finger strum preparation

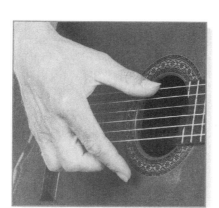

fig. 2   Completion

Chords

When two or more notes are played at the *same time,* it is called a **CHORD.** The notes are placed above and below each other on the music staff and are played together (simultaneously), fig. 1.

There are several techniques used to play chords. You can **STRUM** the strings with a pick or with the fingers. You can **PLUCK** the strings with the thumb and fingers. It is useful to learn all of the various right-hand techniques.

fig. 3 Chord

Basic Strum No. 1

The **STRUM TECHNIQUE** is the easiest to use when you are just beginning to learn how to play chords. Using one of the techniques just described, strum the open 3rd string and then continue *downward* across the 2nd and 1st strings, fig. 2.

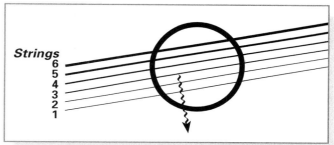

Strings
6
5
4
3
2
1

fig. 4   Strum technique

Left-Hand Position Chord-Playing

The **LEFT-HAND POSITION** will vary slightly with each individual chord. However, there are some basic principles that apply to all chord playing. The *fingernails* must be short so that you can depress the string near the tip of the finger, fig. 5. On many chords, you need to arch the fingers to avoid touching adjacent open strings. To achieve a good sound, and to avoid "buzzing," you need to depress the string as close to the fret wire as is possible. Buzzing occurs when the fretting finger is too far from the fret wire. The *palm* of the hand should not touch or cradle the neck of the guitar and the *thumb* needs to be placed on the back of the neck of the guitar so that it can oppose the fingers in a grip position, fig. 6. How far the thumb extends beyond the back of the guitar depends on the width of the neck and the size of the hand.

fig. 5   Finger position

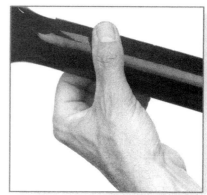

fig. 6   Thumb position

BEGINNING CHORDS

G7 chord–3 strings

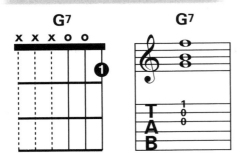

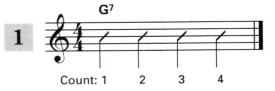

1 Place your index finger on the 1st string, 1st fret—just behind the metal fret. Strum down across the 3rd string toward the 1st string using a pick or a brush strum. Omit (X) the open 4th, 5th and 6th strings.

C chord–3 strings

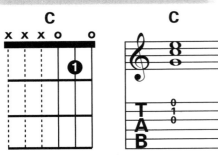

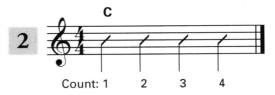

2 Place your index finger on the 2nd string, 1st fret. You must use the pad of the finger in order to avoid touching the 1st string. The fingernail must be short. Omit (X) the 4th, 5th and 6th strings.

As preparation for playing *Marianne,* play exercise 3 using a down-stroke with a pick or a brush strum with the index finger. Gradually eliminate the rests between the chords so that you can move immediately from the C to the G7 chord without any hesitation.

Track 2.1

3

Count: 1 2 3 4   1 2 3 4   Rest (1 2 3 4)   1 2 3 4   1 2 3 4

Marianne

You play the chords. The melody will be played by your teacher or the recording.

Track 2.2 Slowly Traditional

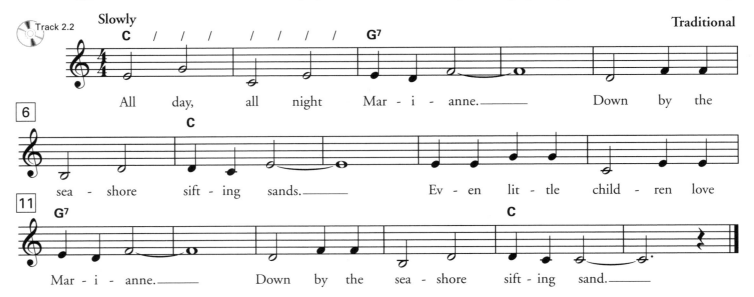

All day, all night Mar - i - anne._____ Down by the

sea - shore sift - ing sands._____ Ev - en lit - tle child - ren love

Mar - i - anne._____ Down by the sea - shore sift - ing sand._____

A7 Chord

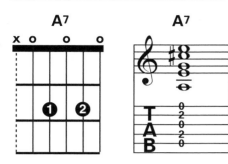

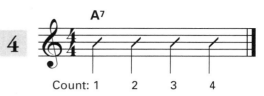

You need to use the pads of your fingers in order to avoid touching the open 3rd and 1st strings. Fingernails must be short. Don't allow the palm of the hand to touch the neck of the guitar. Strum the A7 chord from the 5th string. Omit (X) the 6th string.

D Chord

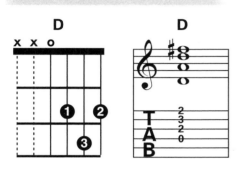

Place the index and middle fingers on the 1st and 3rd strings, 2nd fret and the ring finger on the 2nd string, 3rd fret. You need to arch the 3rd finger in order to avoid touching the 1st string. Strum the D chord from the 4th string. Omit (X) the 5th and 6th strings.

SUBSTITUTE CHORD

If you are having trouble playing the D chord, you could temporarily substitute the D6 chord. Notice that the D6 chord has the same shape as the A7 chord but is located on different strings.

Play exercise 6 as preparation for playing *Tom Dooley* and *He's Got the Whole World.* Practice at a slow speed (tempo) in *real time;* that is, play with a steady beat (avoid the stop and start approach). Work toward playing chord progressions without any hesitation between chord changes. In $\frac{4}{4}$ time, beat **1** should be played louder than 2, 3 or 4. In other words, give emphasis to, or accent (>), the first beat of each measure.

Track 3.1

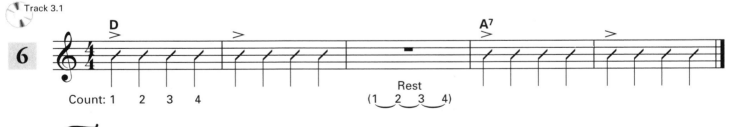

Tom Dooley

Traditional

Track 3.2

He's Got the Whole World

Moderately

Spiritual

He's got the whole world— in his hands.— He's got the whole world—

5

in His hands.—He's got the whole world— in His hands.— He's got the whole world in His— hands.

MORE TWO-CHORD SONGS

Here is a listing of more *two-chord* folk songs that you could attempt to play "by ear" using the D and A7 chords: *Clementine, Down in the Valley, Go Tell Aunt Rhody, Go Tell It On the Mountain, Hush, Little Baby, Merrily We Roll Along, Pick a Bale of Cotton, Rock-A-My Soul, Skip to My Lou.*

G Chord

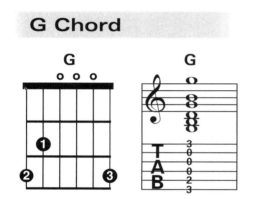

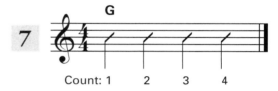

7

Count: 1   2   3   4

Keep the left wrist out and do not allow the palm of the hand to touch the neck of the guitar. Depress the strings just behind the metal fret. Strum the G chord from the 6th string.

SIMPLIFIED CHORD

If you have any difficulty with the regular G chord, try this excellent *simplified* version. Allow the middle finger of the left hand to touch the 5th string. This will *damp* (X) the string (prevent it from sounding).

Play the following drill as preparation for playing *Worried Man Blues, When the Saints Go Marchin' In* and *Amazing Grace.* Always practice in *real time;* that is, play with a steady beat. Work toward playing the chord progression without any hesitation between chords.

8

Count: 1   2   3   4

Rest
(1 2 3 4)

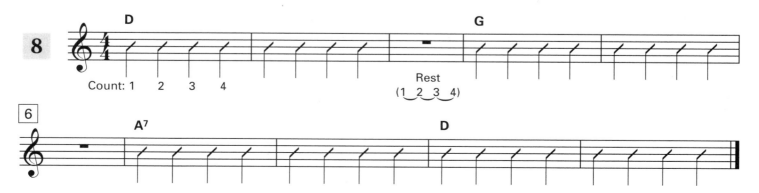

Worried Man Blues

Track 4
Lively   Traditional

It takes a wor-ried man to sing a wor-ried song. It

takes a wor-ried man to sing a wor-ried song. It takes a wor-ried

man to sing a wor-ried song. I'm wor-ried now but I won't be wor-ried long.

When the Saints Go Marching In

Moderately   Spiritual

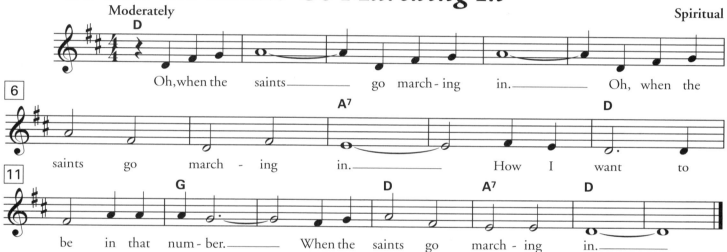

Oh, when the saints go march-ing in. Oh, when the

saints go march-ing in. How I want to

be in that num-ber. When the saints go march-ing in.

Amazing Grace has a $\frac{3}{4}$ **time signature** which organizes the rhythm of the music into three beats in each measure. Slightly accent (>) or give emphasis to the first beat of the measure: **1** 2 3.

Amazing Grace

Track 5
Slowly   Traditional

$\frac{3}{4}$ Time Signature
Count: 1 2 3 1 2 3 etc.

A maz-ing grace, how sweet the sound that

saved a wretch like me. I once was lost but

now am found. Was blind, but now I see.

Review

CHORD CLARITY

While holding the D, G or A7 chord, play each string one at a time to make certain there is no buzzing and that all of the strings are sounding.

WRIST & PALM

The left wrist needs to be out and the palm of the hand should not touch the neck of the guitar.

LEFT ARM

Keep the left elbow in close to your body.

FOREARM POSITION

The right forearm needs to be placed on the edge of the guitar approximately above the bridge base.

STRUMMING

Make certain that you strum the D chord from the 4th string, the G chord from the 6th string and the A7 chord from the 5th string downward.

The following chord progressions have been used in several folk and popular songs.

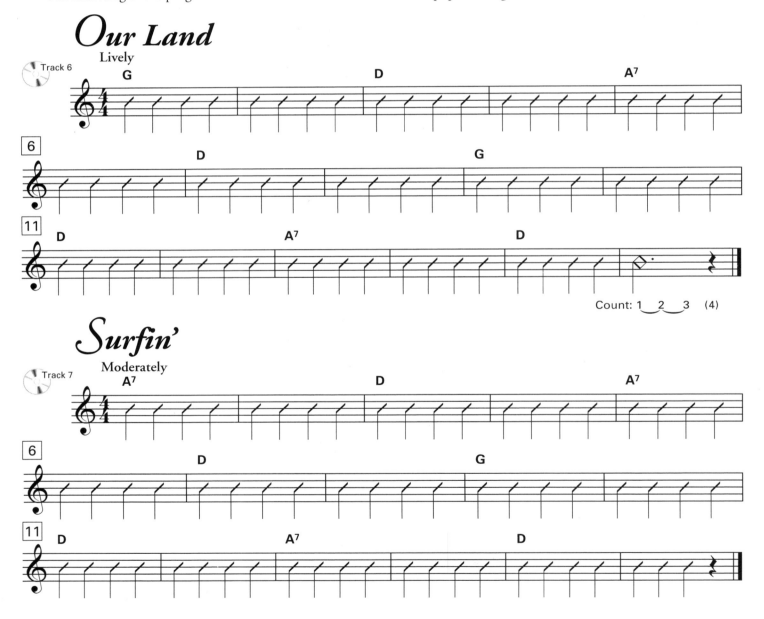

Count: 1 2 3 (4)

MORE THREE-CHORD SONGS

Here is a listing of more *three-chord* songs that you could attempt to play "by ear" using the D, G and A7 chords: *Beautiful Brown Eyes, Blue Tail Fly, Goin' Down That Road Feelin' Bad, Guantanamera, Irene, Happy Birthday,* *Hard, Ain't It Hard, I Walk the Line, Me and Bobby McGee, Red River Valley, She'll Be Coming 'Round the Mountain, Surfin' U.S.A., Swing Low, This Land Is Your Land, This Train.*

Eighth Notes

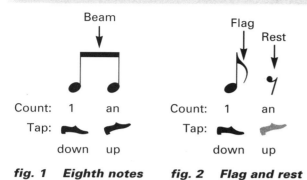

Count: 1   an
Tap: down   up

fig. 1   Eighth notes

Flag
Rest

Count: 1   an
Tap: down   up

fig. 2   Flag and rest

An **eighth note** receives one-half of a count or beat. It can be played on the *down* or on the *up* part of the beat. Eighth notes are often played in pairs and are attached with a *beam,* fig. 1. They can also be written separately, in which case a *flag* is used to indicate an eighth note. Eighth **rests** also receive one-half of a count, fig. 2.

Eighth notes move twice as fast as quarter notes. Count them by inserting the word "an" between the numbers. For example, 1 an 2 an 3 an 4 an, fig. 3.

Count: 1   an   2   an   3   an   4   an
Tap:

fig. 3   Eighth notes

Rhythm guitar parts often use **SLASHES** to indicate eighth-note rhythm patterns. A beam is used to connect the stems of the slashes, fig. 4.

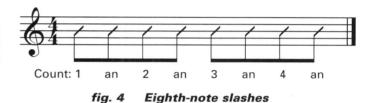

Count: 1   an   2   an   3   an   4   an

fig. 4   Eighth-note slashes

Basic Strum No. 2

PICKSTYLE

Use an up-stroke (V) with the pick on eighth note rhythms that occur on the upbeat (an). Strum the top two or three treble strings (highest sounding strings). Use a minimum of movement. Use a down-stroke (⊓) on downbeats and alternate (⊓ V) down- and up-strokes when you play a succession of eighth-note rhythms.

FINGERSTYLE

Strum down across the strings with the nail of the index finger on downbeats. Keep the hand above the strings. The motion is primarily a finger motion. On upbeats (an), use an up-stroke with the index finger and strum the top two or three strings (treble strings).

Practice the following strum exercise using either the *pickstyle* or *fingerstyle* technique.
Try using this strum on *Our Land* and *Surfin'* introduced on the previous page.

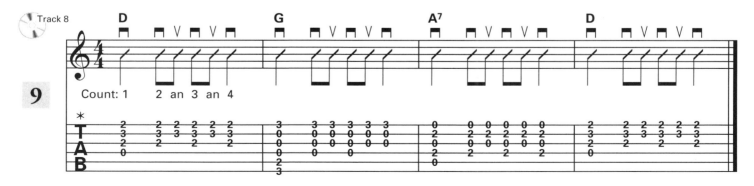

*For a review of TAB, see page 7.

Primary Bass or Root

Various types of accompaniment use the **primary bass** or **root** of the chord. The root or primary bass of any chord is the same as its name: the root of the D chord is D (open, 4th string), the root of the G chord is G (3rd fret, 6th string) and the root of the A7 chord is A (open, 5th string), fig. 1.

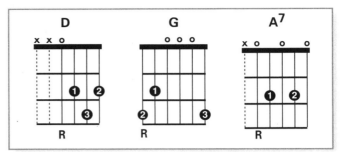

fig. 1   **Primary bass or roots (R)**

Bass/Chord Strum

PICKSTYLE

Use a *down-stroke* with a pick when you pluck the root (R) of the chord. In the down-stroke, the thumb pushes the pick through the string and stops short or slightly above the adjacent (higher in pitch) string.

Exercise 10 is preparation for playing *Bye, Love.*

FINGERSTYLE *(free stroke)*

Pluck the root (R) of the chord with the thumb and allow the thumb to *slightly* pass over the adjacent (higher in pitch) string. The thumb should be rigid (not bent). The primary motion is from the joint nearest the hand. This is called a ***free stroke*** or *tirando* in classical guitar methods.

10

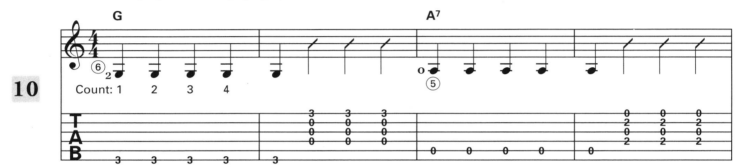

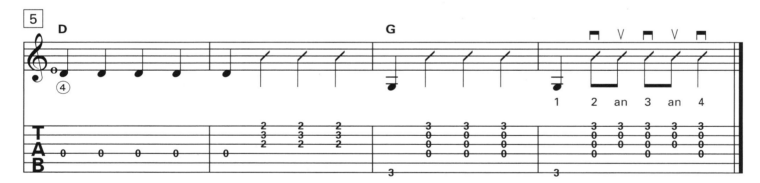

$\mathcal{B}$ye, Love

Pluck the root (R) of the chord on the first beat of each measure. The pattern varies in measures 7 and 9

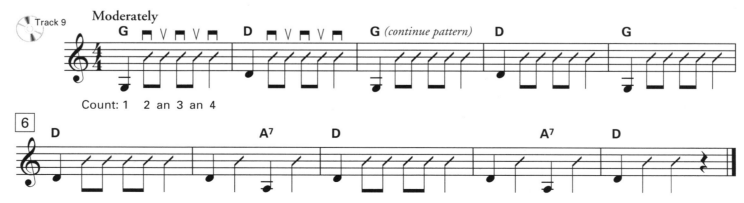

A Chord

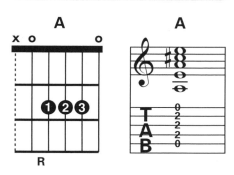

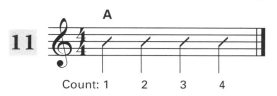

Count: 1   2   3   4

You need to arch the fingers in order to avoid touching the 1st string. The fingernails need to be short. Alternate fingerings are described below. Strum from the open 5th string.

OPTIONAL FINGERINGS

Here are two other commonly used fingerings for the A chord. The first example works best on guitars with narrow necks or if you have large fingers. The second fingering is preferred by some guitarists.

In many of the classic Rock 'n' Roll tunes of the 50's, the A chord is used instead of the A7 chord. The following *Basic Rock/Blues Progression* has been used for many songs: *Whole Lotta Shakin' Goin' On* (Jerry Lee Lewis); *Shake, Rattle and Roll* (Fats Domino); and *Hound Dog* (Elvis Presley). If you play the first four measures twice, you will have the chord progression used in many rock songs such as *Jailhouse Rock* (Elvis Presley) and *Be-Bop-A-Lula* (Gene Vincent).

𝓑asic Rock/Blues Progression

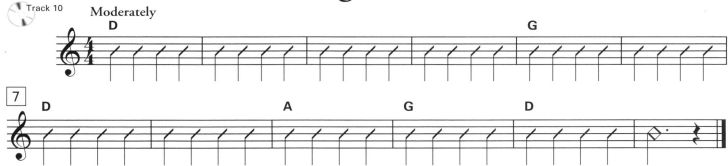

The following is another classic repeating chord progression used in *Twist and Shout* (The Isley Brothers) and many other early rock songs.

And this is a classic chord progression used in such songs as *Louie, Louie* (Kingsmen) and *La Bamba* (Richie Valens).

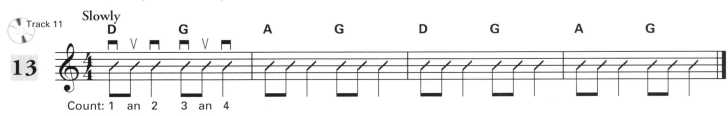

Mute Technique

The **mute technique** is a right-hand technique in which the palm of the hand is used to damp (silence) the strings immediately following a downward strum. Strive for a "chuck" sound. On open strings, play exercise 14 observing the following:

> Strum down across the strings (bass to treble) using either a pick, a brush or scratch strum. Immediately following the strum, allow the palm of the hand to touch the strings in order to silence or *damp* them. The mute needs to be one *continuous* downward motion. The *primary* motion is downward and into the strings.

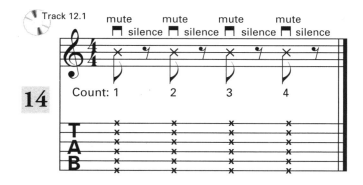

> In exercise 15, strum the open strings on beats 1 and 3, and **mute** the strings on beats 2 and 4. The strum pattern should sound like: chord-chuck *(silence),* chord-chuck *(silence).* When doing the mute, remember to stop the strings from vibrating with the palm of the hand. Mute the strings immediately after the down strum.

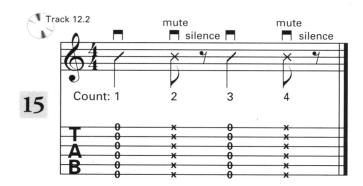

Latin Strum

Add an up-stroke on beats 1**an** and 3**an** and you will have a frequently used **Latin strum.** Try exercise 16 using the open strings, and then play it using the D, G and A7 chords. Strum each of these chords from the root (R) on beats 1 and 3. You only need to strum the top two or three strings on the up-strokes (1**an** and 3**an**).

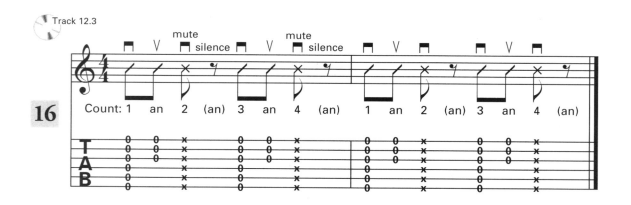

The **Latin strum** works well with songs like *Guantanamera.* Try the following chord progression.

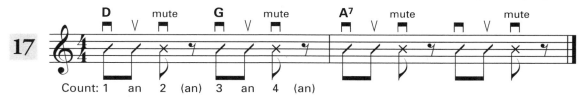

Rock/Mute Strum

Once you have grooved the Latin strum, add an additional up-stroke on 2*an* and 4*an.* This creates a **rock/mute** strum that is quite usable on many popular songs. Accent (>) or give emphasis and stress to the mute on beats 2 and 4. Beats 2 and 4 represent what is referred to as the "back beat" in rhythm guitar playing.

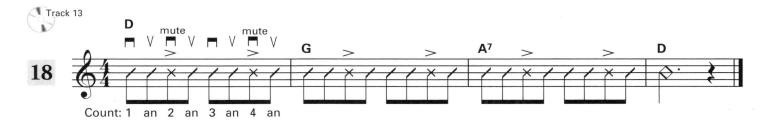

Try using the rock/mute strum on the *Basic Rock/Blues Progression* on page 17.

Chuck Berry wrote many hit songs. In 1958, he wrote the top hit *Johnny B. Goode.* The rock/mute strum works well with this tune. Other Chuck Berry hits include *School Days* and *Roll Over Beethoven.* The following chord progression was used by Berry and many other artists in the 1950s. Play it using the rock/mute strum.

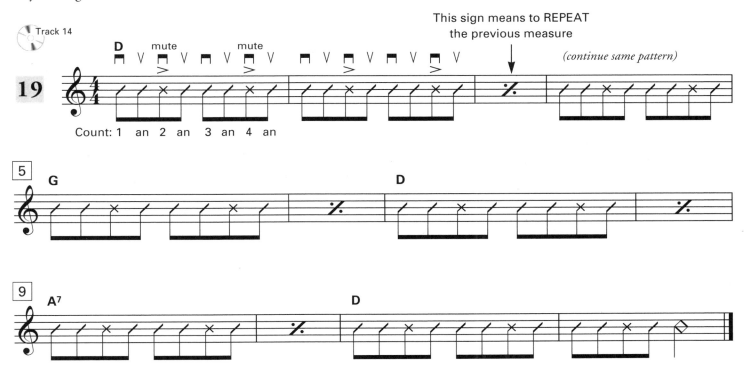

TONALITY (MAJOR KEYS)

Composers frequently work two ways in creating a song: 1) they create a chord progression and then develop the *melody*; 2) they compose a melody and then add the *harmony* (chords).

Harmony can be defined as *chords* and their *progression*. Chords represent the *vertical* analysis of tones and melody the *horizontal* aspect of music. The harmony and melody in much of popular music are derived from the major scale: *do re mi fa sol la ti do,* fig. 1. Chords and melody based on the major scale establish the **TONALITY** (tonal center) or **KEY** (home base) of a song.

This is a key signature which tells you what key you are playing in. For more information, see page 78.

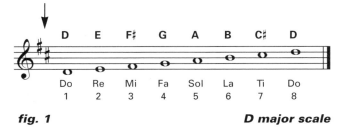

fig. 1   **D major scale**

Key of D

PRINCIPAL CHORDS

The **PRINCIPAL CHORDS** are chords constructed on the first, fourth and fifth degrees of the major scale— *do, fa* and *sol.* In music, roman numerals (I, IV and V) are used to describe them. Many songs stay within the bounds of these three chords. The three chords you have learned thus far, **D, G** and **A,** are the principal chords in the Key of D, fig. 2.

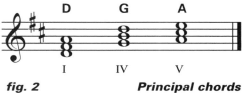

fig. 2   **Principal chords**

ROMAN NUMERAL REVIEW	
I or i = 1	VI or vi = 6
II or ii = 2	VII or vii = 7
III or iii = 3	VIII or viii = 8
IV or iv = 4	UPPER CASE = Major Chords
V or v = 5	lower case = Minor Chords

I CHORD (TONIC)

The most important chord and most frequently used chord in a tonal center or key is the chord built on the first degree of the major scale *(do).* It is a major chord, and it is called the *TONIC* or **I chord.** The I chord is generally used at the beginning and end of a song. In the Key of D, the D chord (I chord) functions as home base.

V CHORD (DOMINANT)

The chord constructed on the fifth note of the major scale *(sol)* is called the **DOMINANT** or **V chord.** It is the most important major chord after the tonic or I chord. Whereas the I chord is stable (inactive), the V chord is unstable (active). It demands movement, most often back to the I chord. The A chord (V chord) or A7 (V7 chord) functions as the **dominant** in the Key of D. It is constructed on the fifth note of the scale. In the D major scale (D E F♯ G A B C♯ D), it is constructed on the fifth note, A.

IV CHORD (SUB-DOMINANT)

The chord constructed on the fourth note of the major scale *(fa)* is a major chord and is called the *SUB-DOMI-NANT* or **IV chord.** It primarily moves to the I chord but very frequently moves to the V chord. The G chord (IV) is the **sub-dominant** chord in the Key of D. It is constructed on the fourth note of the scale. In the D major scale (D E F♯ G A B C♯ D), it is constructed on the fourth note, G.

PLAYING BY EAR

Ear training is an important part of learning how to play the guitar. When you attempt to play easy two- and three-chord songs in the Key of D "by ear," keep in mind the general function of the chords. Learn to anticipate the chord changes in a song. Notice that most songs begin and end with the I chord and that the V or V7 chord seems to demand resolution or movement to the I chord. The IV chord is used to bridge the I and V chords. If you are familiar with any of the following folk songs, try to play the chord changes by ear: **two-chord songs** *Alouette, London Bridge, O Christmas Tree, This Old Man;* **three-chord songs** *Camptown Races, Dixie, Nobody Knows the Trouble I've Seen, You Are My Sunshine.*

Key of G

PRINCIPAL CHORDS

The **principal chords** in the key of G are **G** (I chord), **C** (IV chord) and **D** (V chord). They are constructed on the G scale, fig. 1. Any song played in one major key can be played in any major key. The relationship between the chords remains the same.

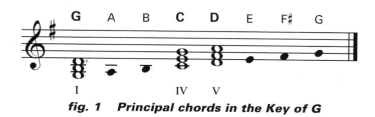

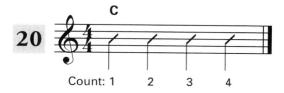

fig. 1   Principal chords in the Key of G

C Chord

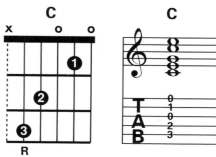

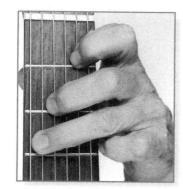

The 3rd fret, 5th string is the root of the C chord. Strum the C chord from the 5th string. Avoid touching the open 3rd string with the second finger. Get up on the pads of the fingers. It is most effective to have the nails trimmed short.

The following *Basic Rock/Blues Progression* was introduced in the Key of D and several practice songs were suggested (see page 17). The same chord progression can be played in the Key of G. It will raise the pitch of the songs, placing them in a higher range.

Basic Rock/Blues Progression

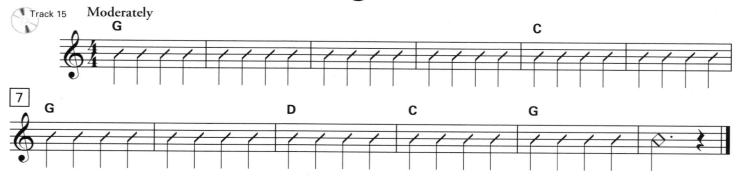

Chord/Mute Strum

Try chord exercise 21 using a chord/mute strum. Accent (>) the mute on beats 2 and 4 (the "backbeat"). This chord progression was common to many 50's songs such as Buddy Holly's *That'll Be the Day* and others.

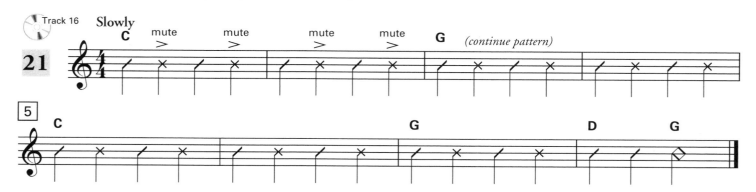

Swing Eighths

Eighth notes are usually played *evenly* with each note receiving ½ of the beat; that is, one eighth note is played on the downbeat and the other eighth note is played on the upbeat. In most rock, Latin and popular music, eighth notes are played in this even manner and referred to as ***straight eighths,*** fig. 1. In other styles of music, eighth notes are not played evenly or "straight." The **shuffle rhythm,** the **blues** and **jazz** are played with *uneven* eighth notes that are referred to as ***swing eighths.*** In swing eighths, the basic beat is subdivided into three parts (triplets); the eighth note played on the downbeat receives ⅔ and the eighth note played on the upbeat gets ⅓ of the beat, fig. 2.

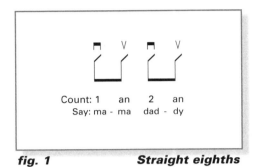

fig. 1   **Straight eighths**

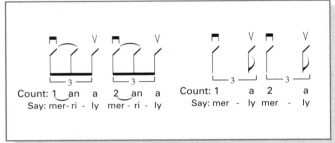

fig. 2   **Swing eighths: the first eighth note is twice as long as the second eighth note.**

The notation required to write swing eighths is rather cumbersome so it has become common practice among rock, jazz and blues musicians and publishers to write straight eighths, and to simply indicate that they are to be performed as swing eighths, fig. 3.

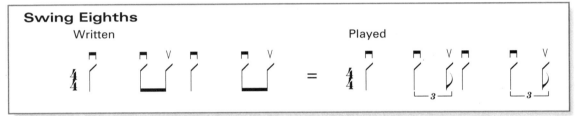

fig. 3 **Swing eighths are written as straight eighths but are played unevenly in a long-short pattern**

SHUFFLE RHYTHM

The shuffle rhythm is used in many rock songs and the blues. Many of Fats Domino's songs use a shuffle rhythm as do many of Stevie Ray Vaughan's. The eighth notes are played as *swing eighths.* Try playing the following **shuffle strum.**

Track 17.1

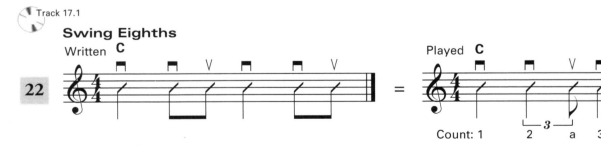

In exercise 23, a ***mute*** is added on beats 2 and 4. Practice this strum on the C and G chords and then play exercise 21 on the previous page with this strum pattern.

Track 17.2

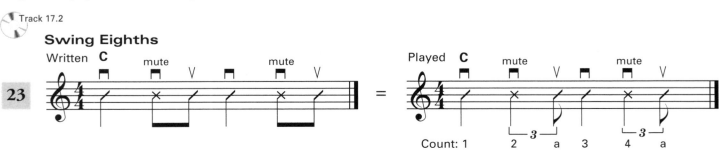

The D seventh (D7) chord is the V7 chord in the Key of G. It is an active chord and usually moves to the I chord (G).

D⁷ Chord

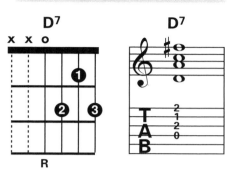

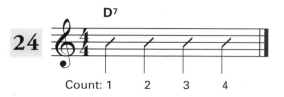

Count: 1   2   3   4

When moving from D7 to G or from G to D7, maintain contact with the third finger, 1st string. Slide the third finger along the 1st string.

Blues Strum

The **blues strum** is a series of *swing eighths* with an accented *mute* on beats 2 and 4. Practice exercise 25 and then use the blues strum on *Just a Closer Walk with Thee.*

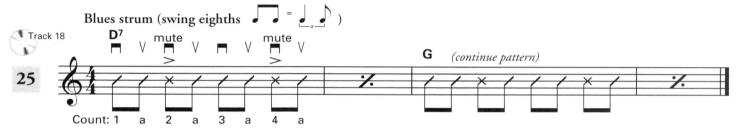

Just a Closer Walk with Thee

MORE THREE-CHORD SONGS

For additional practice in the Key of G, try playing the following songs: *Aloha Oe, (A) Bicycle Built for Two, Give Me That Old Time Religion, Give My Regards to Broadway, Home on the Range, (A) Hot Time in the Old Town Tonight, I Ride an Old Paint, I Was Born Ten Thousand Years Ago, I Wish I Was Single, Jingle Bells, (The) Midnight Special, My Bonnie, O Christmas Tree, Plaisir D'Amour, Red River Valley, Santa Lucia, Study War No More, (The) Wabash Cannon Ball, Worried Man Blues.*

Em Chord

In all major keys, a chord constructed on the sixth degree of the scale *(la)* is a minor chord. Lower case Roman numerals are used to indicate minor chords in this book. The vi chord in the Key of G is E minor (Em), fig. 1.

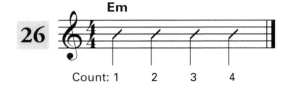

fig. 1.   *The vi chord (Em) in the Key of G*

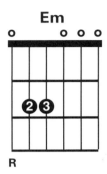  

 The open 6th string is the root (R) of the Em chord. Strum all six strings. Make certain that all of the open strings are sounding.

OPTIONAL FINGERING

Normally it is suggested that you use the second and third fingers to play an Em chord; however, using the first and second finger allows you to leave the second finger down when going to the C chord. The *transportation* between chords dictates the easiest and most logical fingerings.

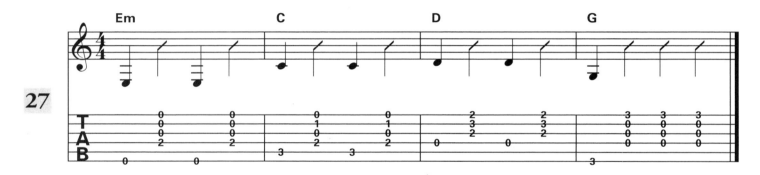

CHORD PROGRESSION I–vi–IV–V

A chord progression that is used extensively in popular music is the I–vi–IV–V chord progression. In the Key of G, the chords are **G** (I), **Em** (vi), **C** (IV) and **D** (V). *Little Darling* (The Diamonds) and *Runaround Sue* (Dion) are examples of songs that use this progression. In exercise 28, use a *down-stroke* with a pick or a *free stroke* with the thumb to play the root (R) of each chord.

REPEAT SIGN

*A **repeat sign** directs you back to the beginning of the music. It is used to avoid writing out repeated measures of music. The sign consists of a double bar with two dots on the inside, facing the measures to be repeated.

Track 20

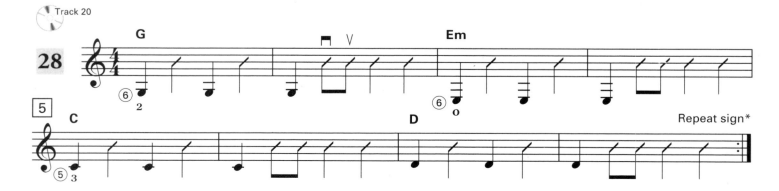

Double Bass/Chord Strum

A variation of the I-vi-IV-V chord progression is used in many other songs such as *Stand By Me* (Ben E. King). Play exercise 29 using a **double bass/chord strum.** Play the primary bass note (root) of each chord twice on beats *1an* and *3an* followed by a down-up strum on beats *2an* and *4an*.

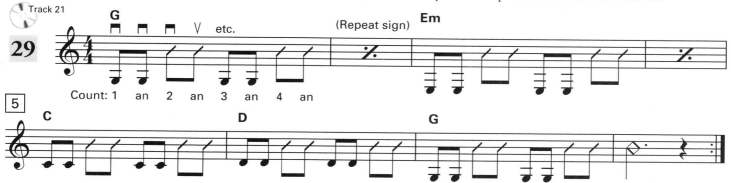

Count: 1   an   2   an   3   an   4   an

Dsus Chord

Generally, a suspended (sus) chord is used to replace a I (tonic) or V (dominant) chord. The D chord functions as the I chord in the Key of D and it is the V chord in the Key of G. The suspended chord is achieved by raising the third of the chord (F♯) by a half step (up to G). It is an active chord that demands resolution. Dsus usually resolves to the D chord.

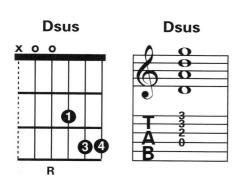

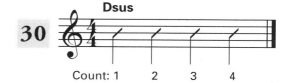

When playing the Dsus chord, add the fourth finger to the 3rd fret, 1st string; continue to keep the second finger on the 2nd fret, 1st string.

The Dsus chord usually moves to or *resolves* to a D chord. For this reason, it helps the *transportation* between these two chords if when playing the Dsus you continue to leave the second finger on the 1st string, 2nd fret.

FIRST and **SECOND ENDINGS** direct you to repeat a section of music. In *Dig It*, play measures 1–16 (which includes the *first ending*); go back to the beginning of the song and repeat measures 1–15; *skip* the first ending and play the *second ending*.

Dig It

Moderately

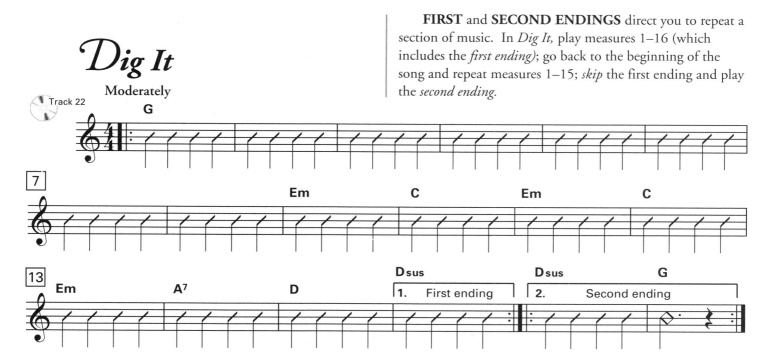

TIE

A **tie** is a curved line that connects the rhythm value of two notes of the same pitch. In rhythm guitar patterns, the tie is often used to connect an upbeat eighth note to a down-beat eighth note. Do not play on the third downbeat. The result is that length and emphasis is given to the upbeat. In music, this is called *syncopation*, fig. 1.

fig. 1   *Syncopated strum*

Syncopated Strum

In playing the **syncopated strum,** it is important that you accent 2*an*. The recommended technique for playing this strum pattern is to use alternating down-up strokes on beats *2 an 3 an*—and to simply *drop out* or *omit* the down-stroke on the third downbeat. Some beginners prefer to use all down-strokes. The syncopated strum, exercise 31, works on many songs such as *I'm Walking* (Fats Domino) and *Take Me Home, Country Roads* (John Denver).

Track 23   **Syncopated strum**

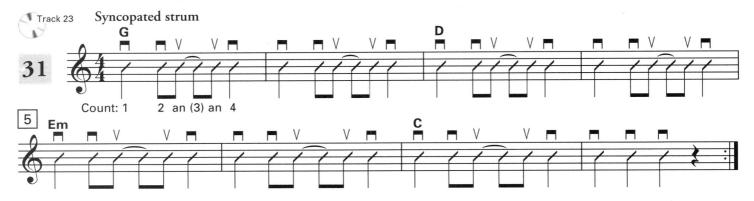

Am Chord

In all major keys, a chord constructed on the second degree of the scale *(re)* is a minor chord. The ii chord in the Key of G is A minor (Am), fig. 2.

fig 2   **The ii chord (Am) in the key of G**

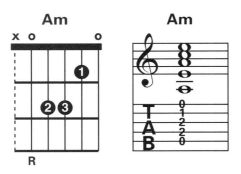

The open 5th string is the root (R) of the Am chord. Strum from the 5th string.

Play exercise 33. When moving from the Am to the D^7 chord, keep the first finger down on the 1st fret, 2nd string since it is common to both of these chords.

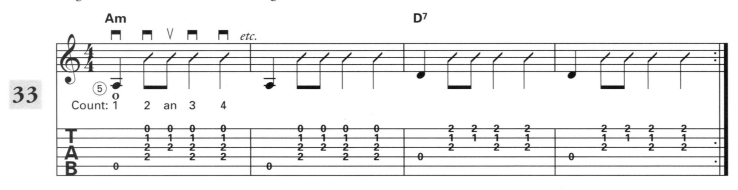

CHORD PROGRESSION I-vi-ii-V

Another chord progression that is used extensively is the I–vi–ii–V chord progression. In the Key of G, the chords are **G** (I), **Em** (vi), **Am** (ii) and **D** or **D7** (V or V7). *Where Have All the Flowers Gone* and *Today* are two examples of songs that use this progression. In exercise 34, use a *down-stroke* with a pick or a *free stroke* with the thumb to play the root (R) of each chord.

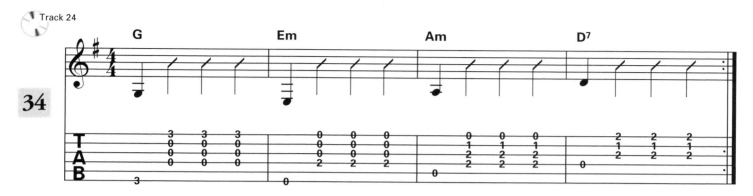

The I-vi-ii-V chord progression was also used in many songs of the 1950s such as *Blue Moon* (Marcels), and *Goodnight Sweetheart* (Spaniels). Play exercise 35.

Here is a nice chord progression that the Beatles and others used in their songs. Try using the **syncopated strum** with the chord progression presented in exercise 36.

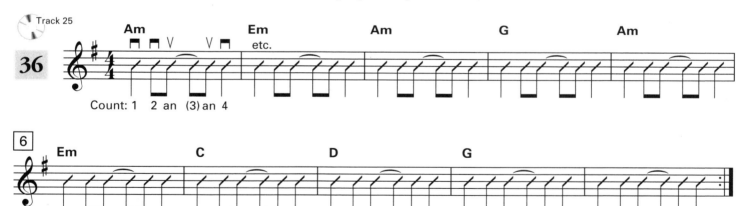

Review

CHORDS

A, A7, Am, C, D, D7, Dsus, Em, G

STRUM TECHNIQUES

Basic strum no. 1, basic strum no. 2, bass/chord strum, mute technique, Latin strum, rock/mute strum, chord/mute strum, blues strum, double bass/chord strum, syncopated strum

THEORY

Tonality, Key of D, Key of G, primary chords, primary bass (roots), swing eighths, shuffle rhythm

CHORD PROGRESSIONS

Basic Rock/Blues, I–vi–IV–V, and I–vi–ii–V

Em Chord

The **E minor** (Em) chord is common to both the Key of G and the Key of D. In the Key of D, the Em chord functions as the ii chord, a chord constructed on the second degree *(re)* of the scale, fig. 1. The ii chord usually moves to the V7 chord (A7).

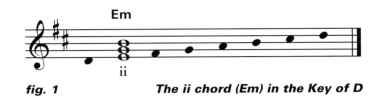

fig. 1   *The ii chord (Em) in the Key of D*

CHORD PROGRESSION ii–V–I (Key of D)

The ii-V-I is a common chord progression used in popular music and jazz. Practice exercise 37. *Don't Be Cruel* (Elvis Presley) and many other songs have used this chord progression.

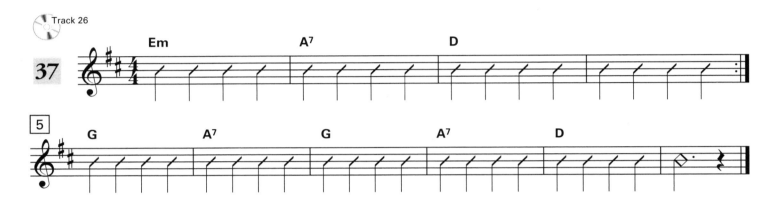

Here is another common use of the Em chord in the Key of D.

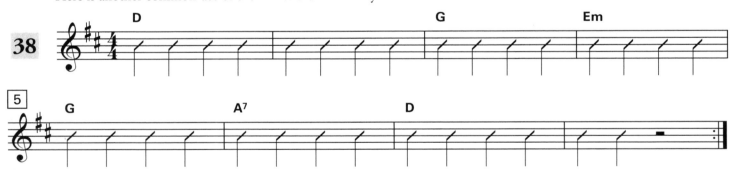

The **bass chord strum** works well on this next chord progression entitled *Help*. Pluck the root (R) of the chord on beats 1 and 3, strum the chord on beats 2 and 4.

Help

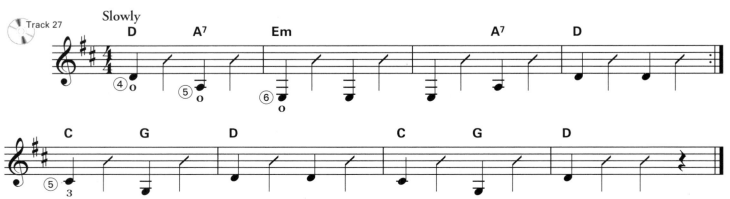

Key of A

PRINCIPAL CHORDS

The **principal chords** in the Key of A are **A** (I chord), **D** (IV chord) and **E** (V chord) or **E7** (V7 chord). They are constructed on the A scale, fig. 1.

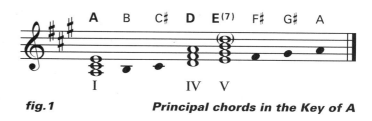

fig. 1   ***Principal chords in the Key of A***

E and E⁷ chords

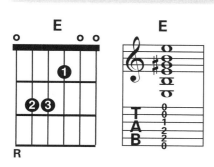

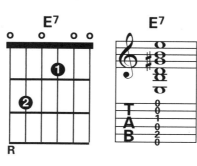

The open 6th string is the root of the E and E⁷ chord. Play exercise 39 using either the E or E⁷ chord.

OPTIONAL FINGERING

The E⁷ chord can also be played by adding the fourth finger to the 2nd string, 3rd fret. This places the seventh of the chord on a higher sounding string which resolves nicely into the A chord.

Here is the *Basic Rock/Blues Progression* in the Key of A.
Kansas City (Carl Perkins) is based on this chord progression.

 Track 28

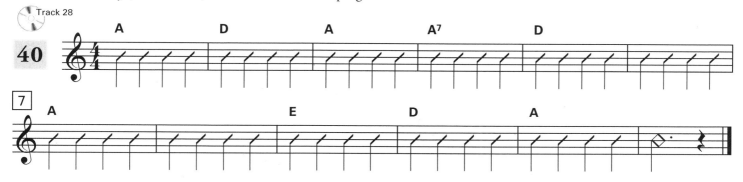

Fats Domino used a shuffle rhythm on *Blueberry Hill.* Try the following chord progression using a shuffle rhythm. Accent or give emphasis to the first and third beats of the measure.

Track 29

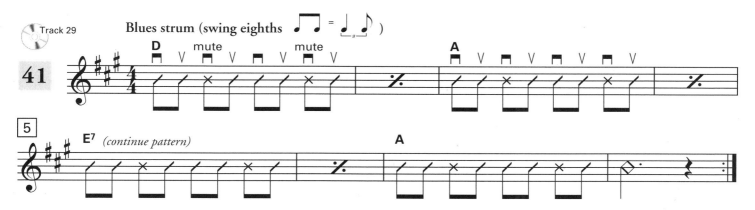

8-Bar Blues

After you have practiced the chord changes in the *8-Bar Blues,* play it with a *blues strum,* exercise 43.

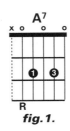

TRANSPORTATION TIP
The easiest way to play the A⁷ chord when it follows the A chord is to lift the second finger, fig. 1.

fig.1.

Track 30

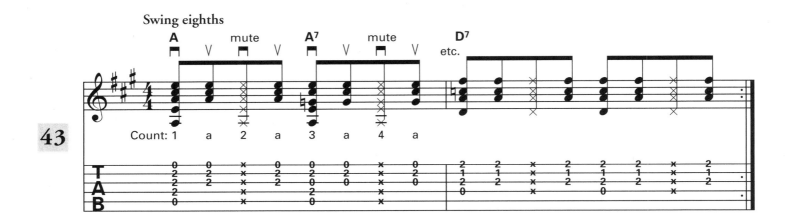

Challenge

ALTERNATE CHORD FORMS

Try the *8 Bar Blues,* using some alternate chord forms. The A and A7 chord, fig. 2 and 3, are located at the 5th fret and contain the open 5th and 1st strings. The D7 and E7, fig. 4 and 5, are *moveable forms.* Notice that the position of the left-hand fingers is similar to the C chord except the fourth finger is added to the 2nd string. Damp the open 1st string with the left-hand index finger. Strum both chords from the 5th string.

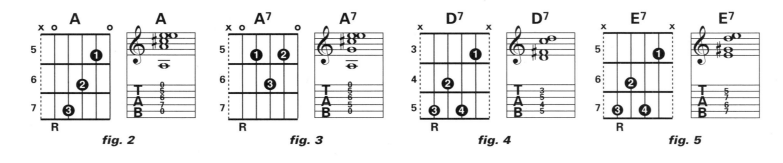

fig. 2   fig. 3   fig. 4   fig. 5

Blues Shuffle in A

The **blues shuffle** in the Key of A is a rhythm guitar accompaniment that uses partial chord voicings with emphasis on the bass strings. Chuck Berry and others have used this accompaniment pattern in their songs. Use down-strokes with a pick on all of the chords. Fingerstyle players can use the index finger or the thumb to strum the chords.

Track 31

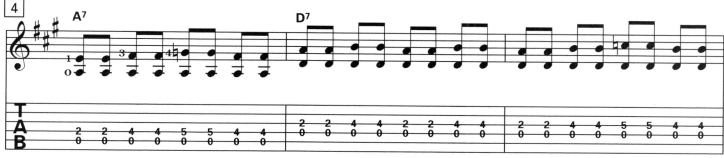

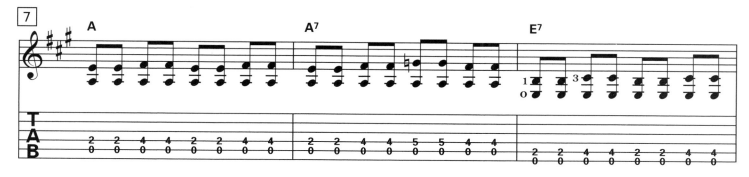

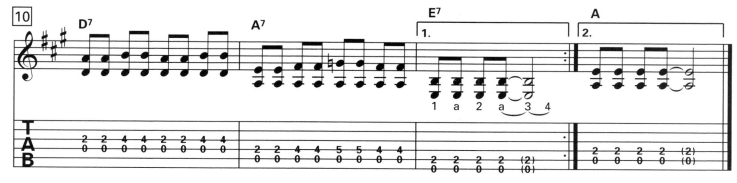

Simile means to continue in a similar manner.

Blues Shuffle

VARIATION

A variation of the blues shuffle pattern can be used on any of the chords in the above chord progression. You can play this variation throughout the progression or use it occasionally for contrast.

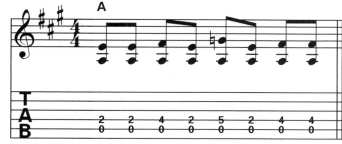

Power Chords

RHYTHM GUITAR

Power chords are two-note chords. They have a root (R) and a fifth (5) and no third. This enables these chords to function as either major or minor chords. The left-hand index finger can be used to *damp* (x) the adjacent (higher in pitch) strings. These chords are usually played with a pick, but fingerstyle players can strum them with the index finger.

The most effective playing technique is to rest the right hand on the bridge and *mute* the strings with the heel of the hand as you strum successive down-strokes. Power chords are associated with the rhythm guitar sound of various rock groups such as The Who, Led Zeppelin, Metallica, Pearl Jam, Green Day and others.

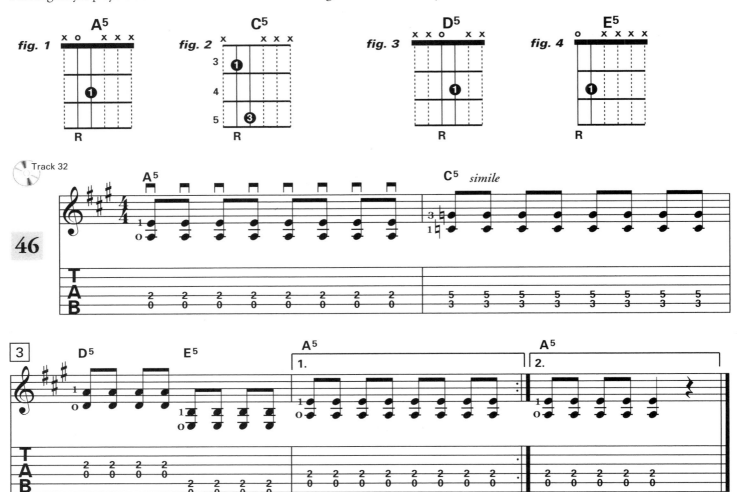

Challenge

MOVEABLE POWER CHORDS

Moveable power chord forms do not contain open strings, and they often double the root (R) of the chord, fig. 6 and 9. Since these are moveable chords, move the D5 chord, fig. 8, to the 3rd fret to play the C5 chord; move the D5 chord to the 7th fret to play the E5 chord. Use these moveable power chord forms on exercise 46.

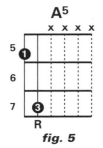

fig. 5

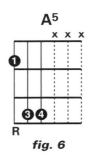

fig. 6

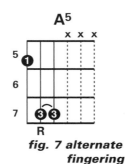

fig. 7 alternate fingering

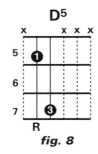

fig. 8

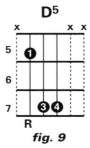

fig. 9

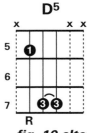

fig. 10 alternate fingering

Key of E

PRINCIPAL CHORDS

The **principal chords** in the Key of E are **E** (I chord), **A** (IV chord) and **B**^{7} (V^7 chord). They are constructed on the E scale, fig. 1.

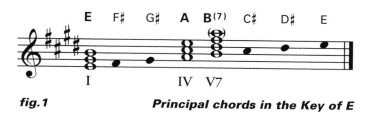

fig.1   ***Principal chords in the Key of E***

B^7 chord

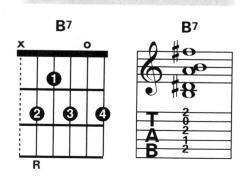

The 5th string, 2nd fret is the root of the B^7 chord. Notice that the first, second and third fingers are placed in the same shape as the D^7 chord except on different strings.

TRANSPORTATION TIP

The B^7 and E chord share a *common* finger. When moving from the B^7 chord to the E chord, or the E to the B^7 chord, *leave* the second finger down.

fig. 2   **OPTIONAL FINGERING**

Finger the A^7 chord with the second and third fingers when moving to and from the E and B7 chords. This will create a smooth chord change.

12-Bar Blues

The **12-Bar Blues** progression has been used in a countless number of songs and there are many variations. Once you can play the chords without hesitation, play the following basic blues progression using the blues strum (page 23), the double bass/chord strum (page 25) and the syncopated strum (page 26).

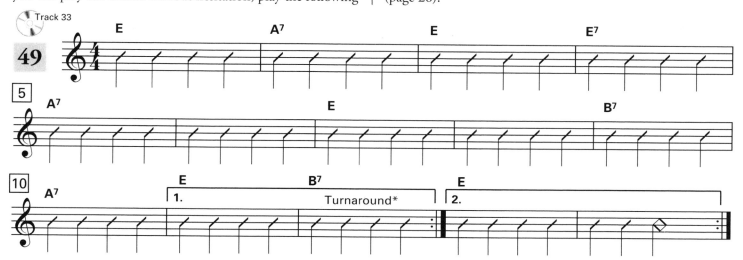

*A *turnaround* is a chord, or group of chords, that takes you back to the beginning.

Blues Technique

SLIDE

It is possible to create some "bluesy" sounds by approaching a chord from a fret above, fig. 1, or from a fret below, fig. 2. Strum the *slide chord* and then **SLIDE** the fingers into the A7 chord.

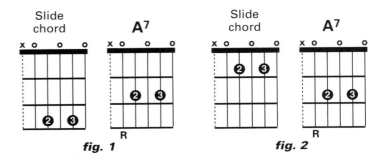

fig. 1   fig. 2

In exercise 50, you need to arrive on the A^7 chord on the first downbeat of the measure. The slide chord is an anticipation of the A^7 chord.

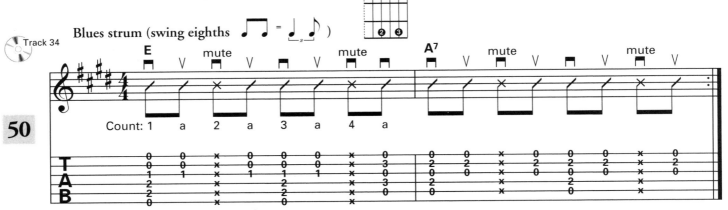

Blues Technique

LIFT

Lift the first finger, fig. 3, or all of the fingers, fig. 4, off of the fingerboard and strum the *lift chord*.

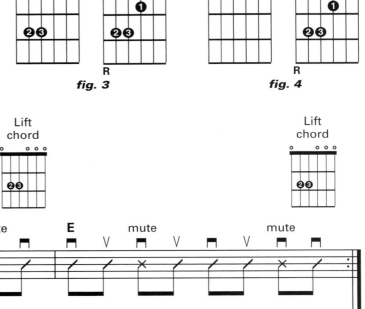

fig. 3   fig. 4

Lift on the upbeat (4a) to play the lift chord. Play the E chord on the first downbeat of the measure.

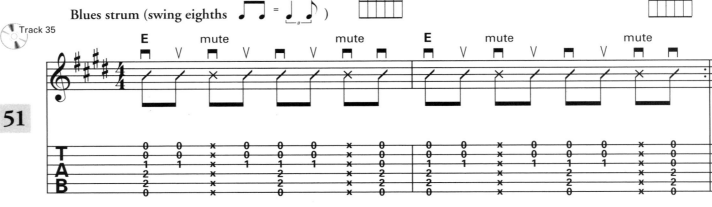

Play the **12-Bar Blues** on page 33 inserting the **slide chord** on the A7 chord and the **lift chord** on the E chord. These techniques add interest and variety to the accompaniment pattern.

Blues Shuffle in E

The **blues shuffle** in the Key of E is somewhat similar to the shuffle introduced on page 31. Use down-strokes in both pickstyle and fingerstyle. Play *swing eighths.*

Challenge

*BLUES SHUFFLE ON B⁷

It requires a long stretch to play the shuffle pattern on the B⁷ chord. Your index finger is on the 5th string, 2nd fret and your ring finger is on the 4th string, 6th fret, exercise 53.

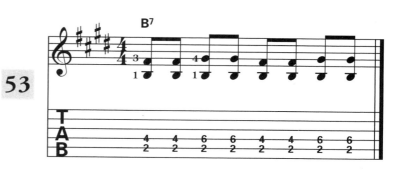

Blues Shuffle

CHORD EMBELLISHMENTS

Chord embellishments are chords that are *extended* beyond the basic three-note major or minor chord. In this example, a fourth note, the sixth or the seventh of the chord, has been added. The E6, E7, A6 and A7 are embellishments of the basic E and A chords. Practice the chords in figs. 1–6 and then play chord exercise 54. Play *swing eighths*. Notice that the shuffle pattern is now in the treble strings.

Add the **MUTE** to beats *2* and *4* in chord exercise 54. Accent, or give stress, and emphasis to the mute. It represents the *backbeat* of the strum pattern.

Sixteenth Notes

Four **sixteenth notes** can be played on a beat or one count, fig. 1. Two notes are played on the *downbeat* and two notes are played on the *upbeat*.

In rhythm guitar playing, sixteenth notes are usually used in combination with eighth notes to create various accompaniment patterns. The two most common patterns are an eighth note followed by two sixteenth notes, fig. 2, and two sixteenth notes followed by an eighth note, fig. 3.

fig. 1   Sixteenth notes   **fig. 2**

fig. 3

Play the following exercises very slowly as in playing a rock ballad. Use *down-strokes* on all eighth notes.

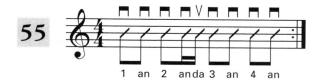

55

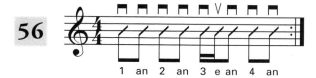

56

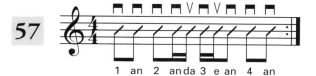

57

Rock Ballad Strum

The **rock ballad strum** works very well on slow songs like *You've Got a Friend* (James Taylor), *I Want to Hold Your Hand* (Beatles) and *Hey Jude* (Beatles). Since the strum is played slowly, down-strokes are normally used on all of the eighth notes. Play exercise 58 slowly. Give emphasis or stress to beats *1* and *3*.

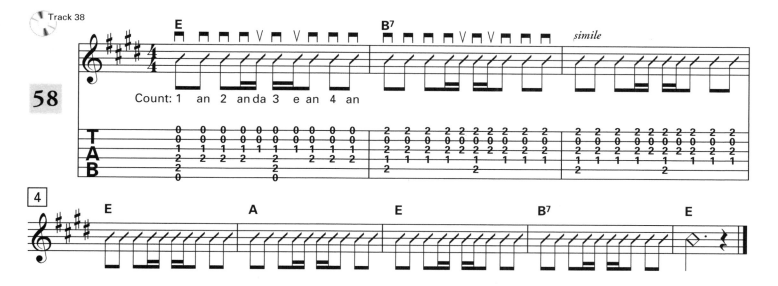

58

VARIATION

A **variation** of the rock ballad strum would be to double bass beats *1 & an*. In fingerstyle, use the thumb to pluck the root of the chord.

59

MINOR KEYS

All major keys and scales have a *relative* **MINOR KEY** and **SCALE**. The relative minor key and scale is constructed on the 6th note of the major scale and thus, shares the same key signature. For example, the **E minor scale** begins on the 6th note (E) of the G major scale and goes up one octave to the next E. This is called the **NATURAL MINOR SCALE.** The key signature for the Key of G (G major) and the Key of Em (E minor) is one sharp (F♯), fig. 1.

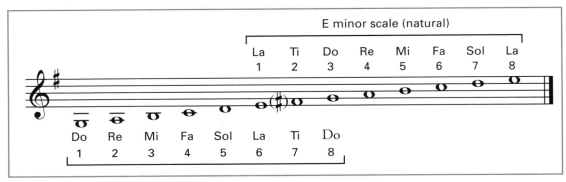

fig. 1
G major scale and relative Em scale

Key of Em

PRINCIPAL CHORDS

In the majority of songs written in a minor key, one alteration is made to the minor scale; the seventh note of the scale is *raised* a **half-step**. This form of the minor scale is called the **HARMONIC MINOR SCALE** since it changes the V chord from a minor chord to a major chord. The V chord now functions as a **dominant** chord and is usually extended to a V7. The **PRINCIPAL CHORDS** in the Key of Em are **Em** (i chord), **Am** (iv chord) and **B7** (V7 chord), fig. 2.

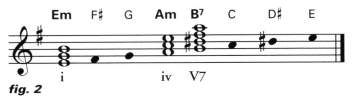

fig. 2

Principal chords in the Key of Em, based on the E harmonic minor scale (raised 7th)

12 Bar Minor Blues

The standard 12 bar **minor blues** has been used in many standard tunes such as *The Thrill Is Gone* (B.B. King), and *Mr. PC* (John Coltrane).

C7 CHORD

In the following MINOR BLUES, exercise 60, the C7 chord is introduced. Finger a C chord and then add the fourth finger to the 3rd string, 3rd fret, fig. 3.

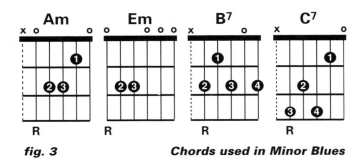

fig. 3   **Chords used in Minor Blues**

Track 39

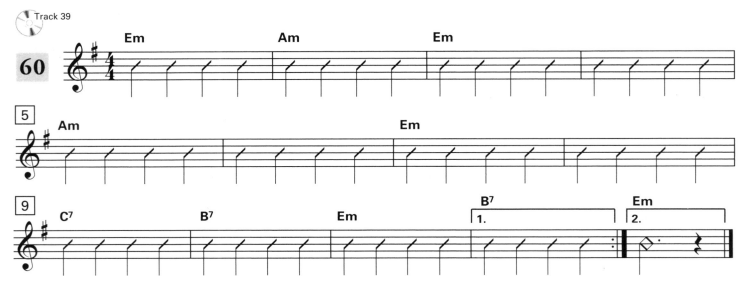

Walking the Bass

Chords can be connected by **walking the bass** from one chord to another. In the following example, the G and C chords are approached from below by a half step. This chord progression can be used for *House of the Rising Sun.*

Track 40

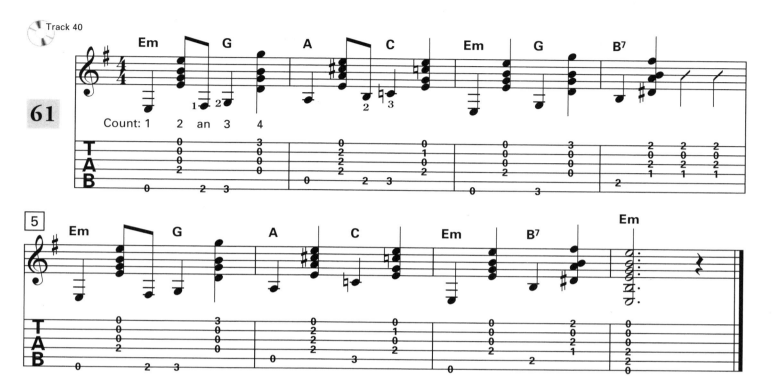

III VI VII Chords in Minor Keys

In minor keys, chords constructed on the third (III), sixth (VI), and seventh (VII) degrees of the *natural* minor scale (no raised seventh) are MAJOR chords. In the Key of Em, **G** is the III chord, **C** is the VI chord and **D** is the VII chord, fig. 1.

fig. 1   *The III, VI and VII chords in the Key of Em*

CHORD PROGRESSIONS i–VII–i & i–VII–VI–V–i

In minor keys, the i chord often moves to the VII chord and then back to the i chord (Em–D–Em). *Scarborough Fair* is an example of this kind of chord movement, exercise 62. *Greensleeves* is a good example of the stepwise chord movement in the i–VII–VI–V–i chord progression, exercise 63.

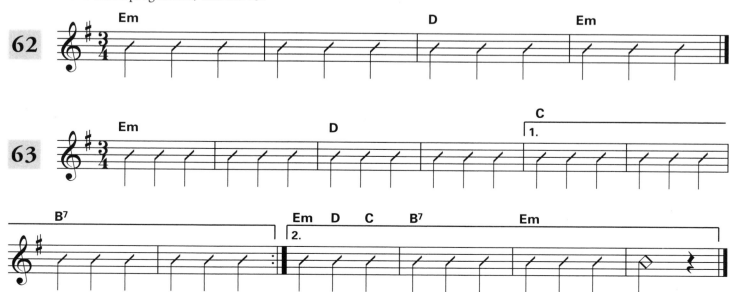

Chord Embellishments

Am⁷ Gmaj⁷ Cmaj⁷

When notes are added to the basic major and minor triads (three-note chords) they are called **EMBELLISHMENTS.** They are extensions of the chord. Embellished chords add *color* to the chord.

The **Am⁷** (A minor seventh), **Gmaj⁷** (G major seventh) and **Cmaj⁷** (C major seventh) are embellishments that are commonly used in jazz, fig. 1. The following chord progression is similar to the chords used in the first part of the standard *Autumn Leaves.*

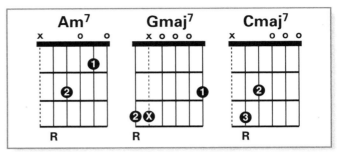

fig. 1   **Embellished chords**

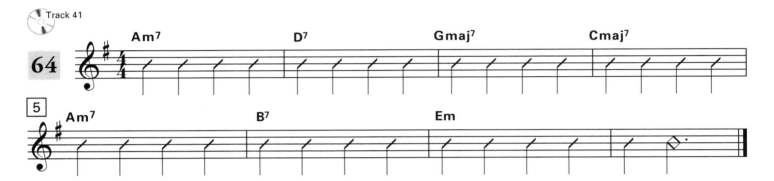

Challenge

F#m7♭5 CHORD

A frequently used embellished chord in the Key of Em, is the chord constructed on the second degree of the scale, **F#m7♭5** (F sharp minor seventh, flat 5), fig. 2. The F#m7♭5 chord usually moves to the B7 (V7) chord. In exercise 65, substitute F#m7♭5 for the Am in measure 4.

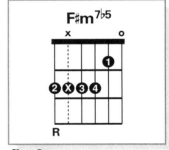

fig. 2

Latin Strum

VARIATION

To play the **Latin strum variation,** simply *drop out* (do not strum) on the second beat. Stress or accent (>) *1an.* Use an alternate down-up-down strum pattern. An optional strum pattern is to play two down-strokes in a row.

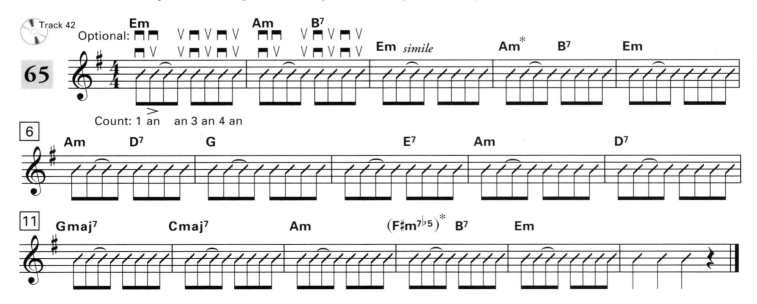

*OPTIONAL: Either play the Am chord here or substitute the F#m7♭5 chord:

Key of Am

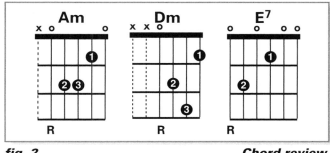

fig. 1   **Principal chords in the Key of Am, based on the A harmonic minor scale (raised 7th)**

PRINCIPAL CHORDS

The Key of Am (A minor) is the *relative* minor key to the Key of C (C major). The **PRINCIPAL CHORDS** in the Key of Am are **Am** (i chord), **Dm** (iv chord) and **E7** (V^7 chord), fig. 1.

Dm Chord & Chord Review

The Am chord (page 26) and the E^7 chord (page 29) have already been introduced. Add the Dm chord and you can play the principal chords in the key of Am, fig. 2.

fig. 2   **Chord review**

Principal chords in a minor key function in the same manner as the principal chords in a major key. The iv (Dm) most frequently moves to the i chord (Am). Its second most frequent progression is to the V^7 (E^7) chord. Practice the following chord exercise.

III VII Chords in Am

In minor keys, the VII chord, a chord constructed on the 7th degree of the scale (natural minor scale—no raised 7th) and the III chord are major chords. In the Key of Am, the VII chord is G and the III chord is C, fig. 3. This next chord progression is in the style of the one used in *You've Got a Friend* (James Taylor).

fig. 3   **The III and VII chords in the Key of Am**

Track 43

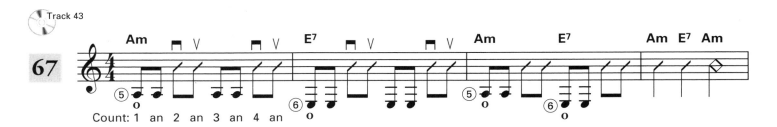

Count: 1 an 2 an 3 an 4 an

In the Key of Am, the **F** chord functions as the VI chord. Since it contains no open strings, it is a more difficult chord to play. There are, however, some simplified versions that are more "guitar friendly." The three-string F chord and the small bar F chord are easier than the full bar version.

F Chord

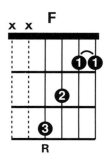
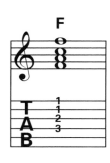

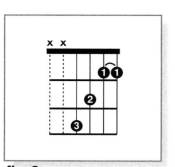

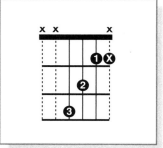

fig. 1
Build the F chord from the 4th string.

SMALL BAR

The **small bar F CHORD** requires the first finger of the left hand to cover (fret) two strings—the 1st and 2nd strings. The pressure needs to be on the side of the index finger. Build the chord from the 4th string, fig. 1. Once you have placed the index finger on the 2nd string, roll the index finger toward the nut of the guitar as you cover the 1st string, fig. 2. Since the strings are lower and the frets are narrower at the 5th fret of the guitar, practice the small bar chord in 5th position. The name of a position on the guitar is determined by the location of the left hand index finger. If your index finger is on the 5th fret, you are in 5th position, fig. 3.

fig. 2
Roll the index finger onto the 1st string.

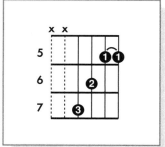

fig. 3
Practice the small bar in 5th position.

Challenge

FULL BAR F CHORD

The **Full Bar F** chord requires you to cover (fret) all six strings with the index finger. To develop the ability to play the full bar, I recommend that you practice it at the 5th fret. At the 5th fret, the strings are closer to the fingerboard and the frets are closer together. This makes it easier to form the full bar chord.

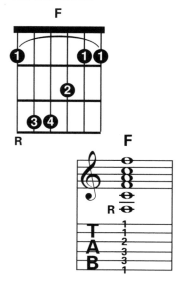

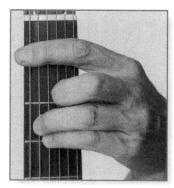

Begin by placing the index finger across all of the strings at the 5th fret. The index finger must be straight. Slightly arch the wrist out (away from the neck) and place the thumb opposite the index finger in a grip position. The palm of the hand should not touch the neck of the guitar, fig. 4. Now add the second, third and fourth fingers, fig. 5. When you can play this chord form at the 5th fret, move it down to the 1st fret to play the full bar F chord.

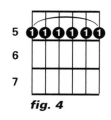
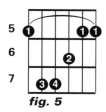

fig. 4   fig. 5

Love Story and *Sunny* are popular songs in the Key of Am that use the F chord (VI chord).
Play the following chord exercises. Use either the small or full bar F chord.

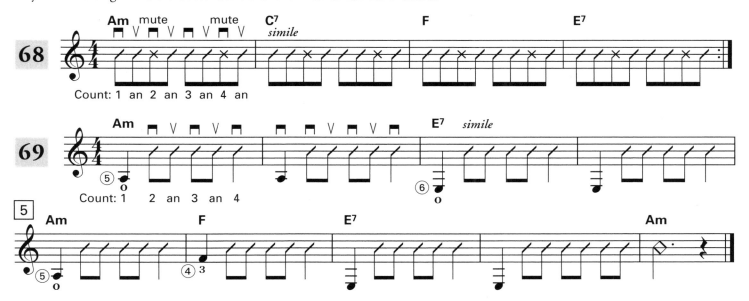

More Embellished Chords

Am⁷ Dm⁷

In the JAZZ MINOR BLUES, exercise 70, the i and iv
chords are usually embellished. In the Key of Am, the Am (i)
becomes an **Am⁷** and the Dm (iv) becomes a **Dm⁷,** fig. 1.

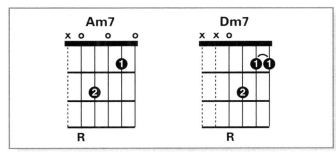

fig. 1   **Embellished minor chords.**

Track 44

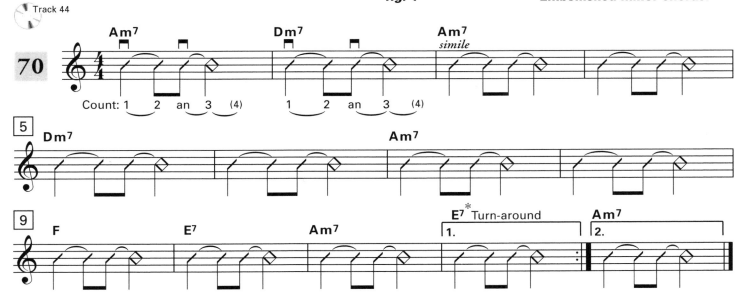

Challenge

*Bm11 CHORD

An embellished ii chord is often used in the ii-V⁷ chord
turn-around in jazz. Try substituting a Bm11 to E⁷ chord
progression in the first ending of the JAZZ MINOR
BLUES, fig. 2. Give each chord two beats.

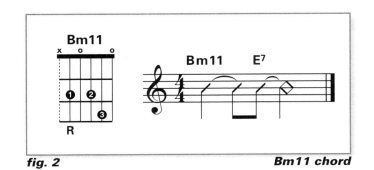

fig. 2   **Bm11 chord**

FINGERSTYLE ACCOMPANIMENT

The basic fingerstyle hand position is described on page 86. Study this material before attempting the various exercises presented on this page. The basic fingerstyle hand position is used to play various plucking and arpeggio (broken chord) accompaniment patterns. While some of these patterns can be played pickstyle, it is recommended that you learn these fingerstyle techniques.

The basic fingerstyle hand position is described on page 86.

RIGHT-HAND FINGER SYMBOLS

p and T = thumb
i or 1 = index
m or 2 = middle
a or 3 = ring

Plucking Pattern in ¾

On the open strings, play exercise 71. The thumb plucks the root (R) of the chord and the fingers pluck the treble strings (3rd, 2nd and 1st strings). Repeat this exercise several times.

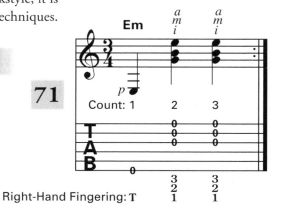

71

Right-Hand Fingering: **T**

Dmaj⁷ D6 A⁷sus Chords

Down in the Valley contains several embellished chords: Dmaj⁷, D6 and A⁷sus, fig. 1, 2 and 3. Practice the plucking **pattern in ¾** on each chord before attempting the song. The thumb plucks the root (R) of the chord.

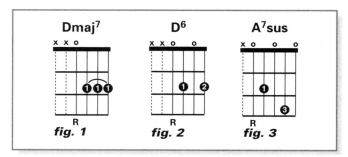

Down in the Valley

Track 45   Slowly   Traditional

Scarborough Fair

Traditional

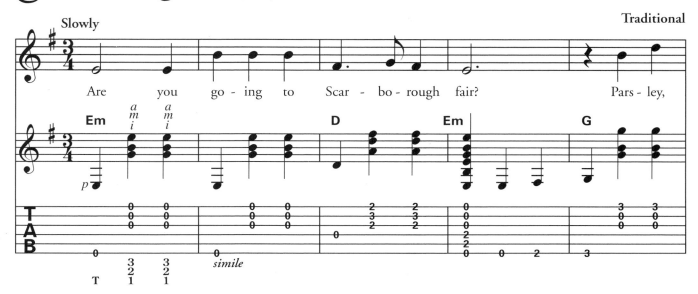

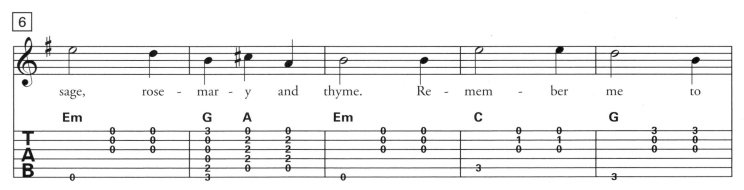

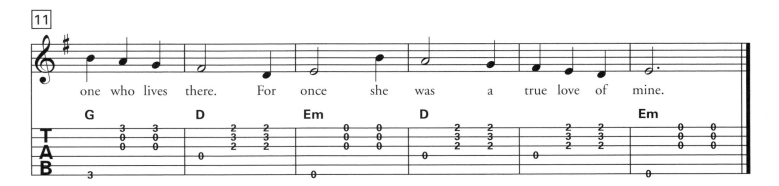

Plucking Pattern in $\frac{4}{4}$

On the open strings, try playing exercise 72. The thumb plucks the bass on beats *1* and *3* and the fingers pluck the treble strings (3rd, 2nd and 1st strings) on beats *2* and *4*. Repeat this exercise several times. Try using this accompaniment pattern on the chord changes to the *House of the Rising Sun*, page 94.

72

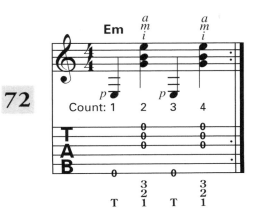

Plucking Arpeggio in 4/4

An arpeggio is a *broken chord* pattern. Notes of the chord are plucked and allowed to sustain or ring into the next note. The thumb usually plucks the root (R) of the chord on beat *1* and alternates to the fifth (5) of the chord on beat *3*. Practice exercise 73 and then play *Sometimes I Feel Like a Motherless Child*. In measures 7, 8 and 9, play half of the pattern for each chord. The thumb plucks the root of the chord.

73

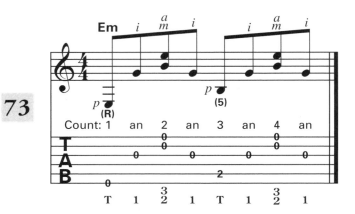

Sometimes I Feel Like a Motherless Child

Track 46   Slowly   Spiritual

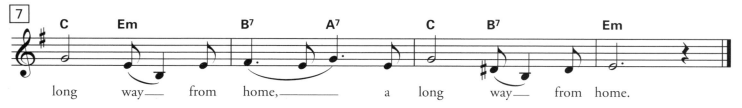

Plucking Arpeggio Variations in 4/4

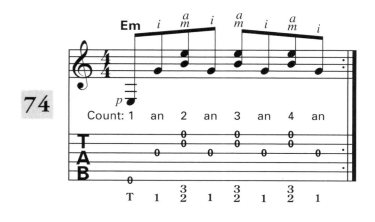

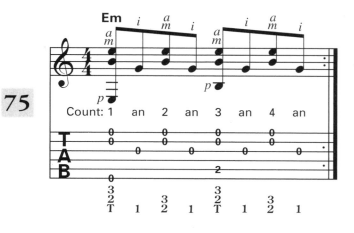

Plucking Arpeggio Pattern in 3/4

Here are two common plucking patterns. Try using the accompaniment pattern notated in exercise 76 on *Down in the Valley*, page 44. The thumb plucks the root (R) of the chord. Play *Silent Night* using the pattern notated in exercise 77.

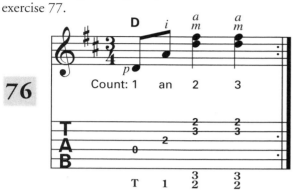

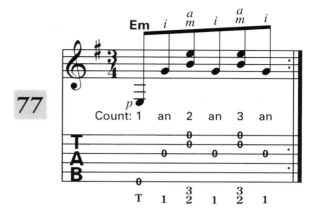

Silent Night

Slowly

Traditional

Si – lent night,   ho – ly night,   All is

calm,   all   is   bright.   'Round   yon   vir – gin

Moth – er   and   child.   Ho – ly   in – fant so   ten – der and

mild.   Sleep   in   heav – en – ly   peace.___

Sleep___   in   heav – en – ly   peace.___

Arpeggio Pattern in ¾

In the arpeggio pattern, each tone is plucked individually. The thumb *(p)* plucks the root (R) of the chord. Practice this pattern on the open strings (Em chord). In measures 9 and 24 of *Greensleeves,* you need to pluck each chord.

Greensleeves

Track 47

Traditional

What Child Is This? *(The Christmas version of Greensleeves)*

What child is this, who laid to rest on Mary's lap is sleeping?
Whom angels greet with anthems sweet, while shepherds watch are keeping?
This, this is Christ the King, whom shepherds guard and angels sing.
Haste, haste to bring Him laud, the Babe, the Son of Mary.

*A double bar like this indicates the end of a section.

Arpeggio Patterns in $\frac{4}{4}$

Review the basic fingerstyle hand position on page 86. It is important to *plant* the fingers in position before you begin the **arpeggio pattern.** The thumb plucks the root (R) of the chord. Play exercise 78 and then play exercise 79. In measure 3, walk the bass from the G chord to the Em chord.

78

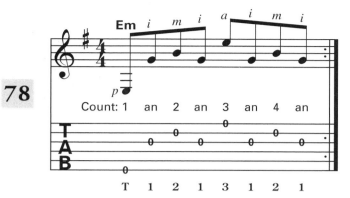

Arpeggio Patterns

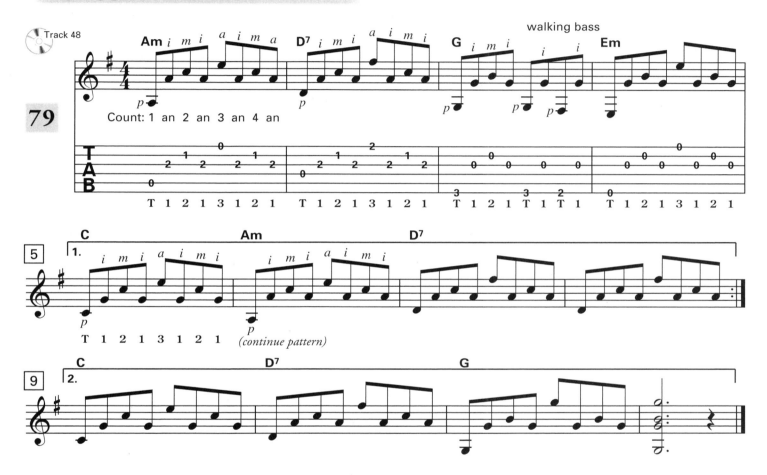

Variations in $\frac{4}{4}$

In the following arpeggio patterns, the thumb plucks the bass string on beats *1* and *3*. For additional variety, alternate the thumb to the fifth (5) of the chord on beat *3*. The Basic Chord Chart on page 57 indicates the root (R) and fifth (5) for the various chords.

80

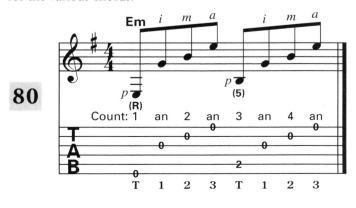

81

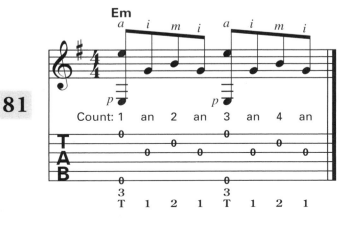

Key of C

PRINCIPAL AND SECONDARY CHORDS

The **principal chords** in the Key of C are **C** (I chord), **F** (IV chord), and **G7** (V7 chord). The **SECONDARY CHORDS** are **Dm** (ii), **Em** (iii) and **Am** (vi). These chords are constructed on the C scale, fig. 1.

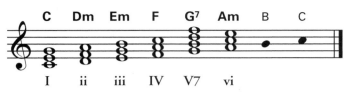

fig. 1   ***Principal and Secondary Chords in the Key of C, based on the C major scale***

G⁷ Chord

There are two commonly used open string forms of the G⁷ chord. The root of the chord is located on the 6th string, fig. 2 and 3.

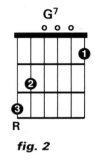
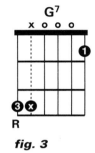

fig. 2   *fig. 3*

Review

F CHORD

Review the F chord on page 42. The small bar F, fig. 4 and the full bar F, fig. 5, require the index finger to cover more than one string. You could substitute one of the simplified forms, fig. 6 and 7.

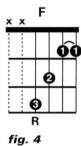
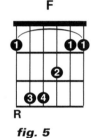
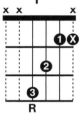
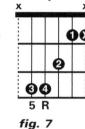

fig. 4   *fig. 5*   *fig. 6*   *fig. 7*

The I-vi-ii-V⁷ chord progression has been used in many songs such as *Where Have All the Flowers Gone?* and *Unchained Melody.* In pickstyle, play the root of the chord on beat *1* and use alternate strumming on beats *2 3 4.* You can play example 83 in one of two ways. Fingerstyle— play the basic arpeggiation pattern Pickstyle—play the following pattern:

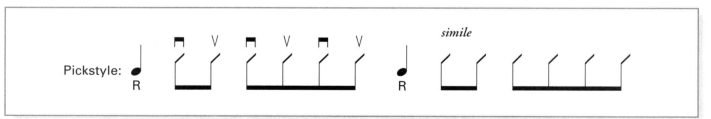

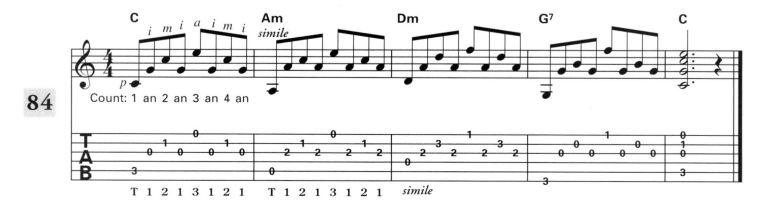

Here's a chord progression in the style of one used by the Beatles.

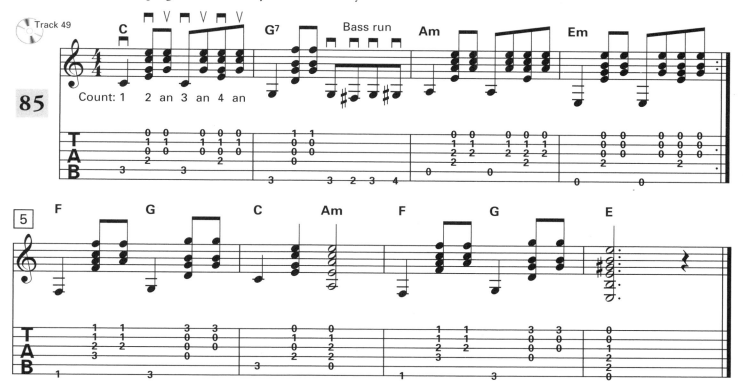

Am add9 Chord

To play the **Am add9 chord,** finger Am and simply pick up the first finger allowing the open 2nd string (B) to sound, fig. 1. The strum pattern is indicated for pickstyle players in exercise 86. Fingerstyle players should pluck measures 1 and 2 and then use a combination of plucked bass notes and index finger strumming for the rest of the chord progression. You'll recognize this progression as similar to the changes used in *Song from MASH.*

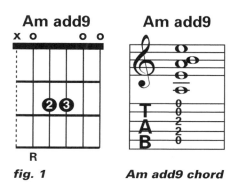

fig. 1   **Am add9 chord**

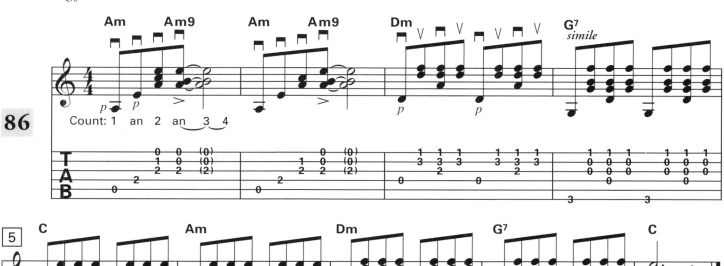

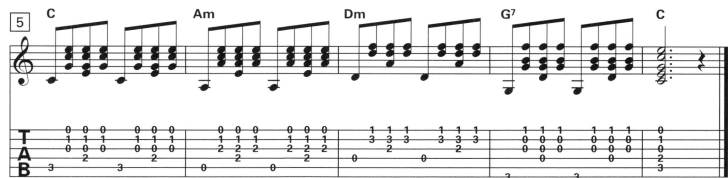

BASS NOTES

Roots and Fifths

The **ROOT (R)** of a chord is the same as the name of a chord; that is, D is the root of the D chord. The strongest voicing of a chord is to play the root at the bottom and to strum chords from the root.

When developing an accompaniment bass, the root is the *primary bass* and is generally played on the first beat of the measure. The most frequently used *alternate bass* is the **FIFTH (5)** of the chord. For a D chord, A is the fifth of the chord—D E F♯ G **A** (1 2 3 4 **5**). You need to memorize which bass strings represent the root (primary bass) and fifth (alternate bass) of any chord. This task is simplified by the fact that the root and fifth are the same for major, minor and dominant seventh chords that share the same alphabetical name. For example, the D, Dm and D7 chords all have the same root (D) and fifth (A).

Alternating Bass/Chord Strum

Practice the root and fifth of each of the following chords using a bass/chord pattern, exercise 87. When playing the C and B7 chords, it is necessary to move the fretting finger from the root of the chord to the fifth of the chord. There are several options for the F chord.

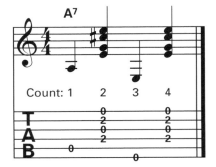

87

Another good way to practice the root and fifth bass notes is to play the I–IV–V⁷–I chord progression in major keys and the i–iv–V⁷–i chord progression in minor keys. In $\frac{4}{4}$ time, play each chord twice using the **alternating** bass/chord strum. Notice that the A, A⁷ and Am chords give you the choice of using the fifth (5) of the chord on either the 6th string or the 4th string.

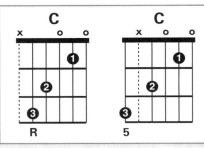

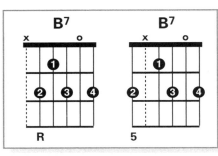

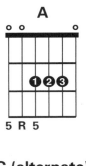  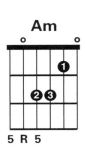

 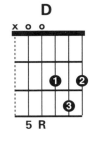 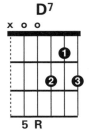 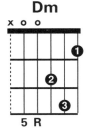 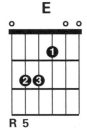 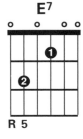

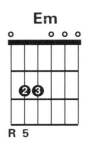 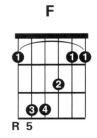 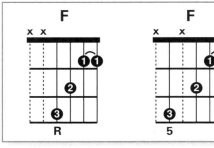 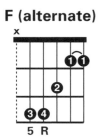 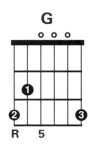

The **alternating bass/chord strum** is used a lot in country and country-rock type songs. The following chord progressions move through several chords and are similar to the patterns found in *Big, Bad Leroy Brown* (Jim Croce) and *Hotel California* (Eagles).

Chord Name/Bass Note

Em/D♯ CHORD

A common practice in voicing chords is to indicate a particular note to be played in the bass. This is done by adding a SLASH (/) after the chord name and then by writing the name of the bass note. For example, Em/D# means to play an Em chord with a D# in the bass, fig. 1.

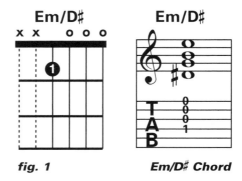

fig. 1   **Em/D♯ Chord**

The following chord progression has been used in songs such as *This Masquerade* (George Benson), *Feelings,* and *My Funny Valentine* (standard). The chord/slash notation indicates the bass line movement. It can be played either pickstyle or fingerstyle.

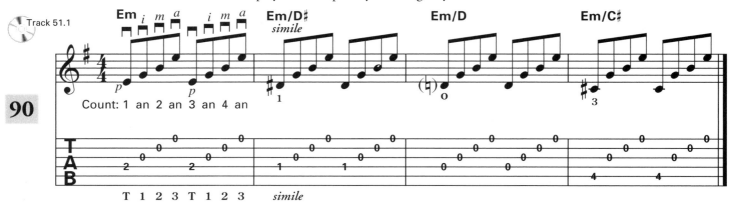

The following chord progression has also been used in a countless number of popular songs and standards including *Yesterday* (Beatles), *Love Story* and *Mr. Bojangles.*

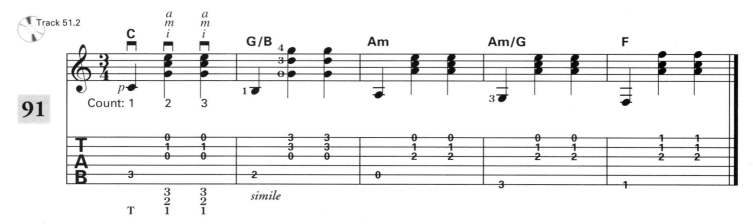

Challenge

The following descending stepwise bass line chord progression has been used in many popular songs. *Annie's Song* (John Denver), *Vincent* (Don McLean), and *Mr. Bojangles* (Nitty Gritty Dirt Band) are just some examples.

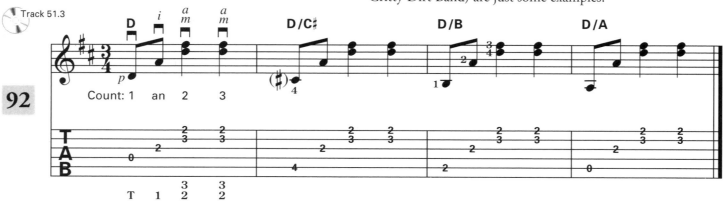

More Chord Embellishments

MAJOR CHORDS that function as I or IV chords can be extended to become major 6th, major 7th, add⁹ or suspended chords. For example a C major chord could be extended *(embellished)* to become a C⁶, Cmaj⁷, Cadd⁹ or Csus, fig. 1.

Embellishments can be used whenever you want to add additional color to a chord. Jazz musicians are always looking for ways to embellish chords and to discover substitute chords that will enrich the harmony of a song. There has been an increased use of embellished chords in popular and rock music.

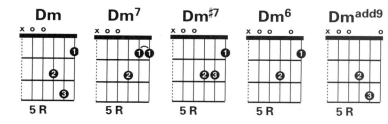

fig. 1

Major chord embellishments

MINOR CHORDS can also be embellished. For example, a Dm can become Dm⁷ (D minor 7th), Dm#⁷ (D minor sharp 7th), Dm⁶ (D minor 6), or Dm add⁹ (D minor add 9), fig. 2.

The following *embellished* chord progression has been used in many popular songs.

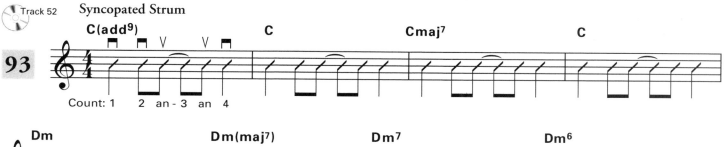

fig. 2

Minor chord embellishments

Track 52   **Syncopated Strum**

93

Challenge

MAJOR CHORDS that function as V type chords have many embellishments. The most common are the V⁷ and the V⁷sus—see pages 57 and 59. Jazz musicians extend and alter the V chord in many *colorful* ways; for example, a G⁷ chord could become a G⁹, G⁷#⁹, G⁷♭⁹, G⁷#⁹♭⁹, G⁷#⁵, G⁷♭⁵, G¹¹, G¹³. Most of these chords are more advanced *moveable chords* and are beyond the scope of this book. There are, however, a few "guitar friendly" dominant 7th, flat 5 chords, fig. 3.

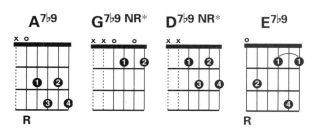

fig. 3.

Dominant 7th, ♭5 embellishments

CHORD PROGRESSION V-I

94

*NR = no root

Chord Review

GUITAR FRIENDLY CHORDS AND KEYS
Guitar friendly **CHORDS** are chords that contain *open* strings. These are the easiest chords to play on the guitar. Guitar friendly **KEYS** are keys where the majority of the chords are *open* chords. In the **MAJOR KEYS** of D, G, A, and E and the **MINOR KEYS** of Am and Em, the **principal chords** (i, iv, V7) are all open string chords.

The Key of D is a good key to begin with since the I, IV and V7 chords are quite playable for beginners. The Key of G is perhaps the most overall guitar friendly key since the **PRINCIPAL** and **SECONDARY** chords, except the iii (Bm), are open string voicings. The F chord (IV chord) in the Key of C makes this key difficult for beginners even though the rest of the principal and secondary chords are open string chords.

Chords that do not contain open strings are more difficult to play and are not considered guitar friendly. However, the advantage they have is that they are MOVEABLE. They can be played anywhere on the neck of the guitar. Some moveable chords require learning the small bar or grand bar technique. In order to play in the Key of C, you must learn the F chord which is a moveable major chord. To play many of the secondary chords, you need to learn moveable minor and minor seventh chord forms.

The following chart includes the **PRINCIPAL** and **SECONDARY CHORDS** in the guitar friendly MAJOR and MINOR KEYS.

PRINCIPAL and SECONDARY CHORDS Guitar Friendly MAJOR keys					
I	ii	iii	**IV**	**V^7**	vi
D	Em	F♯m	**G**	**A^7**	Bm
G	Am	Bm	**C**	**D^7**	Em
A	Bm	C♯m	**D**	**E^7**	F#m
E	F♯m	G♯m	**A**	**B^7**	C#m
C	Dm	Em	**F**	**G^7**	Am

PRINCIPAL and SECONDARY CHORDS Guitar Friendly MINOR Keys						
i	ii7♭5	III	**iv**	**V^7**	VI	VII
Am	Bm7♭5	C	**Dm**	**E^7**	F	G
Em	F♯m7♭5	G	**Am**	**B^7**	C	D

Bass Notes

ROOTS AND FIFTHS
As you review the chords on the **BASIC CHORD CHART,** memorize which string in all chords represents the **ROOT** (R) and the **FIFTH** (5). In general, strum chords from the root of the chord. The root of any chord is the *primary* bass note and the fifth is the *alternate* bass note. Many accompaniment patterns in pickstyle and fingerstyle use alternating bass patterns.

Basic Chord Chart

PRINCIPAL CHORDS in seven keys.
Strum from the **root** (R). The alternate bass is the **fifth** (5).

KEY OF D

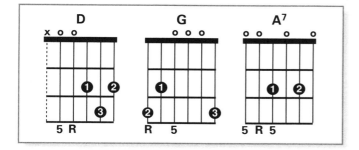

KEY OF G

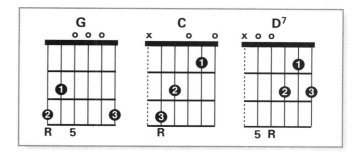

KEY OF A

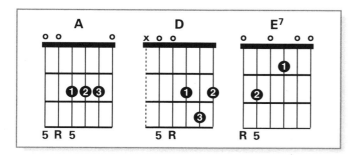

KEY OF E

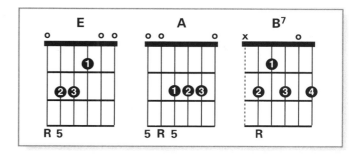

KEY OF C

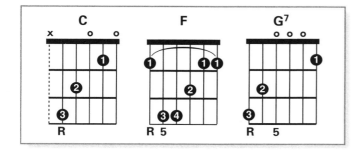

KEY OF Am

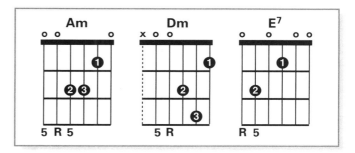

KEY OF Em

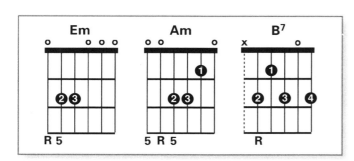

ALTERNATE FINGERINGS

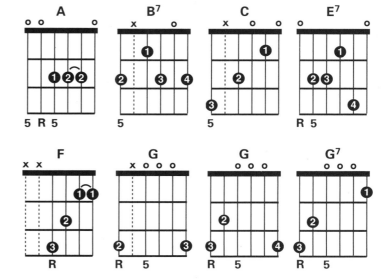

Basic SECONDARY MINOR CHORDS

Basic ii, iii and vi chords. Simplified versions are included for some chord forms.

Am	Bm	Bm	C#m	Dm	Em
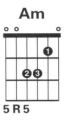	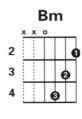	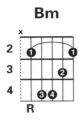	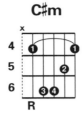	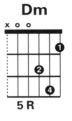	

F#m	F#m	Gm	Gm	G#m	G#m
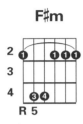	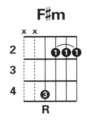	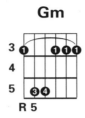	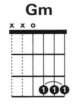	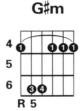	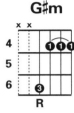

Basic SECONDARY MINOR SEVENTH CHORDS

Secondary minor chords are often *extended*. Simplified and alternate versions are included for some chord forms.

Am⁷	Bm⁷	Bm⁷	Bm⁷	C#m⁷	C#m⁷	Dm⁷
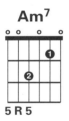	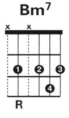	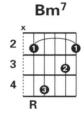	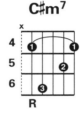	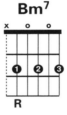	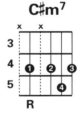	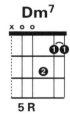

Em⁷	Em⁷	F#m⁷	F#m⁷	Gm⁷	Gm⁷	G#m⁷	G#m⁷
	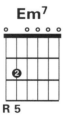	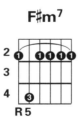	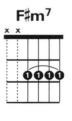	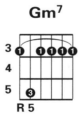	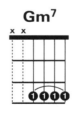	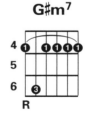	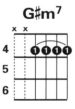

Basic MAJOR SEVENTH and MAJOR SIXTH CHORDS

These are *color* chords that usually function as *extended* I and IV type chords.

Amaj⁷	Cmaj⁷	Dmaj⁷	D⁶	Fmaj⁷	Gmaj⁷	G⁶
	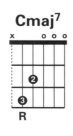	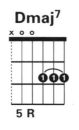	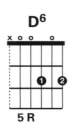	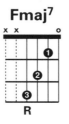	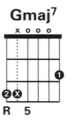	

Basic SUSPENDED CHORDS

Suspended chords are altered major chords. The third of the chord is raised or *suspended* one half step.
They function as I or V^7 type chords and resolve back to the unaltered major or dominant 7th chord.

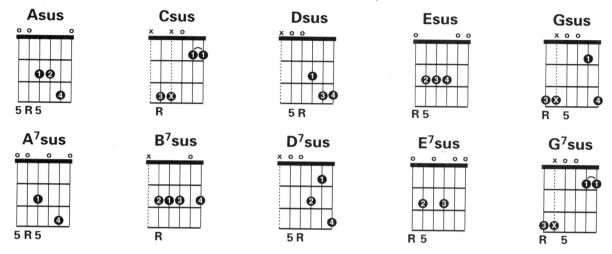

Basic add9 (add2) CHORDS

A major 9th (or 2nd) is added above the root of the
chord to produce the add^9 chord. It is an important *color*
chord that adds interest, variety and tension. It can be used
wherever an increase in color is desired.

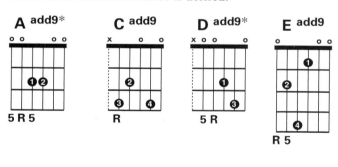

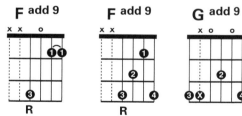

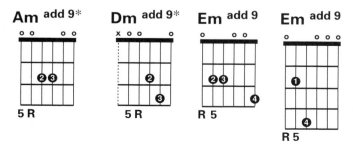

Basic CONNECTING CHORDS

CHORD/BASS

To indicate a bass note other than the root of the chord, a
slash (/) and the name of the note is added after the chord
name. These chords usually function as I type chords and
move to either the IV chord or the IIm chord.

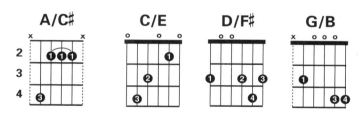

DIMINISHED 7th CHORDS

These chords are generally used to connect ascending
stepwise movement. They usually connect the I to the ii
chord or the V to the vi chord. Any note in the chord can
function as the root (R). Except for the A♯dim^7, all of these
forms are moveable.

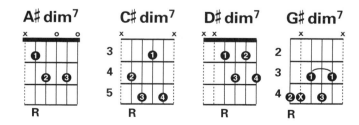

*If there is no third, major and
minor add^9 chords are the same.

MOVEABLE CHORDS

6th String Root Chords

MAJOR, MINOR, DOMINANT 7th

The **6th String Root Chords** are derived from the open E chord forms. They are made *moveable* through the use of the bar technique.

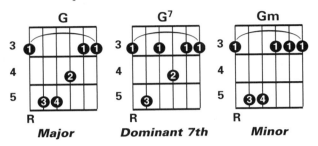

G	G⁷	Gm
Major	*Dominant 7th*	*Minor*

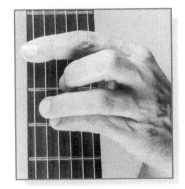

When playing all **full bar** chords, there should be slightly more pressure on the side of the index finger (away from the fret and toward the nut of the guitar). Place the thumb opposite the index finger.

The following chart will help you locate and identify moveable **ROOT 6TH STRING CHORDS.**

NOTE NAME Sixth String ⑥	E	F	F♯/G♭	G	G♯/A♭	A	A♯/B♭	B	C
FRET	Open	1	2	3	4	5	6	7	8

5th String Root Chords

MAJOR, MINOR, DOMINANT 7th

Most of the **5th String Root Chords** are derived from the open A chord form. The bar technique with the index finger and the third finger bar technique are needed to play many of these chords.

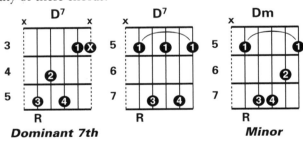

D⁷	D⁷	Dm
Dominant 7th		*Minor*

To play the moveable **Dm** (D minor) **chord,** bar the 5th fret with your index finger. You do not need to cover the 6th string. The pressure on the index finger should be on the side of the finger nearest the nut of the guitar.

The moveable **D chord** requires a *third finger bar* technique. Place the third finger on the 4th, 3rd, 2nd and 1st strings. Damp (X) the 1st string by arching the finger. Now place the index finger on the 5th string. The pressure on the third finger needs to be on the side of the finger toward the fret (just the opposite of the full bar technique). To assist in helping you roll the third finger toward the fret, place the thumb below (toward the nut) rather than opposite the index finger.

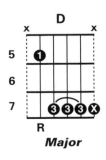

D
Major

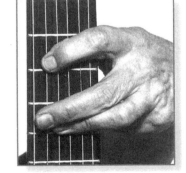

The following chart will help you locate and identify moveable **ROOT 5TH STRING CHORDS.**

NOTE NAME Fifth String ⑤	A	A♯/B♭	B	C	C♯/D♭	D	D♯/E♭	E	F
FRET	Open	1	2	3	4	5	6	7	8

Principal Chords

MOVEABLE

When used together, moveable **root 6th string** and **root 5th string** chords enable you to play the **PRINCIPAL CHORDS** in any key. Practice the **Principal Chords** in the keys of G, C, Am and Em.

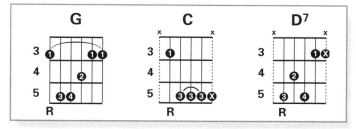

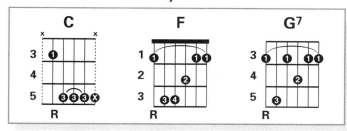

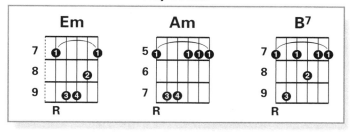

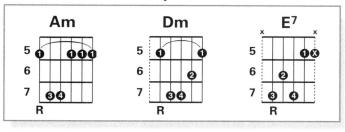

Major Sixth and Seventh Chords

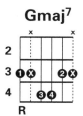
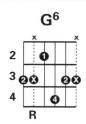
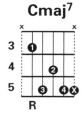
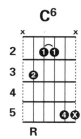
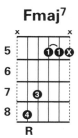
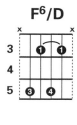

Minor Seventh Chords

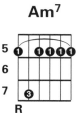
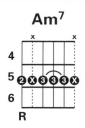
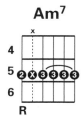
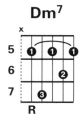
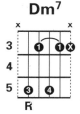
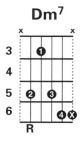

Dominant Ninth Chords

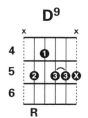
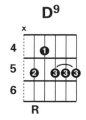
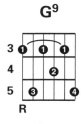

The name of a MOVEABLE chord is determined by where the root is located on the 5th or 6th string. Use the charts on page 60 to locate and name the *moveable* **MAJOR 6th, MAJOR 7th, MINOR 7th** and **DOMINANT 9th** chords.

SECTION TWO
Learning to Read Music

Playing Techniques

The playing techniques used for playing **PICKSTYLE** and **FINGERSTYLE** melody or *lead* are described here. Except for classical guitarists, most guitar players learn both styles.

Pickstyle

Pickstyle guitar players use a **PICK** to pluck or *stroke* the strings. Review page 8 for a recommendation on pick size and shape, and a description of how to hold it.

RIGHT HAND POSITION

There are three commonly used hand positions: 1) free floating, 2) fanning the fingers, and 3) resting the palm of the hand on the strings behind the bridge. In the free floating position, the middle, ring, and little fingers are curled into the hand. They follow the movement of the thumb and index finger as the hand moves from string to string, fig. 1. Some guitarists fan the fingers and allow the little finger to skim the pick guard, fig. 2. For more stability or for special effects, the palm of the hand can lightly rest on the strings just behind the bridge, fig. 3.

fig. 1   Free floating position

fig. 2   Fanning the fingers

fig. 3   Resting the palm

DOWN-STROKE

The **down-stroke** (⊓) is the basic stroke used in pickstyle. In the *down-stroke,* the thumb pushes the pick through the string, stops short of the next string and immediately returns to the starting position. Use an economy of motion. Only follow through enough to finish picking the string. The angle of the pick to the strings should be fairly upright, fig. 4.

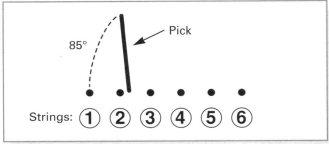

85° ← Pick

Strings: ① ② ③ ④ ⑤ ⑥

fig. 4   **Pick angle**

UP-STROKE

The **up-stroke** (∨) is used on eighth notes that occur on the upbeat (an). Eighth notes are discussed in detail on page 82. In the *up-stroke,* the index finger pushes the pick through the string. Only follow through enough to finish picking the string and then return to the starting point. Alternate (⊓ ∨) *down-* and *up-strokes* are used when you are playing a succession of eighth notes.

Fingerstyle

Place the forearm on the edge of the guitar just above the bridge base. Make a fist with your hand. Now open the hand. Keep the fingers in a natural curve. The knuckles should be above the treble strings (strings 3, 2 and 1). Place the thumb on the 5th string. Keep the thumb rigid. Place your index finger on the 1st string, fig. 1 and 2.

fig. 1   *Hand position*

fig. 2   *Thumb position*

REST STROKE

The **rest stroke** is used to play single-note melodies. In this stroke, the index (*i*) or middle (*m*) finger comes to rest on the adjacent (lower sounding) string.

Plant your index finger on the 1st string and your thumb on the 5th string, fig. 3. *Push* the index finger through the string toward the 2nd string. The index finger comes to rest on the 2nd string, fig. 4. The *primary motion* should originate at the joint nearest the hand.

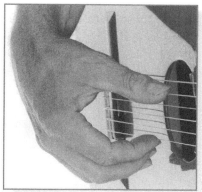

fig. 3   *Preparation*

fig. 4   *Completion*

ALTERNATE the index (*i*) and middle (*m*) fingers when you are playing a melody or a single series of notes.

Left-Hand Position

NOTE PLAYING

An excellent way to develop a good **LEFT HAND POSITION** is to begin by making a fist without bending the wrist. Now bring the hand up to the neck of the guitar and place the fingers on the fingerboard. The wrist should be straight, the fingers curved and the thumb should oppose the fingers in a "grip" position, fig. 5. Most guitarists find their maximum strength when their thumb opposes a spot located between the first and second fingers, fig. 6. Depress the string as close to the fret wire as is possible. Avoid cradling the guitar between the thumb and fingers.

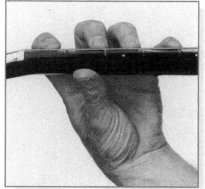

fig. 5   *Finger position*

fig. 6   *Thumb position*

NOTE READING PREPARATION

Rote exercises are helpful in developing *music reading readiness.* Do not begin the note playing exercises on page 66 until you complete these two pages of **NOTE READING PREPARATION.** Review the *music fundamentals* presented on pages 6 and 7.

You need to be able to play single notes on open strings with a pick *(down-strokes)* or with the fingers *(rest strokes)* before you deal with reading music. Review these right-hand playing techniques on pages 62 and 63. Initially, you need to focus on establishing good playing techniques and on producing a good tone.

Play exercises 1–3 on the open 1st (highest sounding) E string using either pickstyle or fingerstyle techniques. Each note gets four counts *(whole notes).* **Pickstyle.** Play all of the notes with a *down-stroke.* **Fingerstyle.** Use a *rest stroke* with the index (*i*) and middle (*m*) fingers as indicated. In classical guitar methods, the rest stroke is called an *apoyando.* The goal is to be able to *alternate* between *i* and *m.* Repeat each exercise several times.

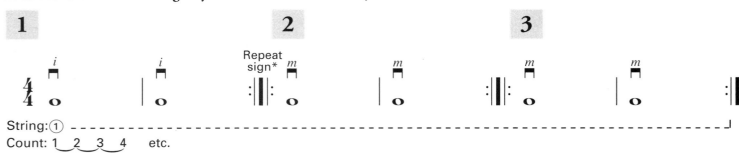

Before going on, play exercises 1–3 on the 2nd and 3rd strings.

Practice all of the following exercises on the open *treble* strings (1st, 2nd and 3rd strings). These exercises combine whole-note and half-note rhythms. A half note receives two counts. When exercises 5 and 6 are repeated, you need to start on *m.* The idea is to always *alternate* the fingers. Begin the repeat of exercise 5 with the middle finger.

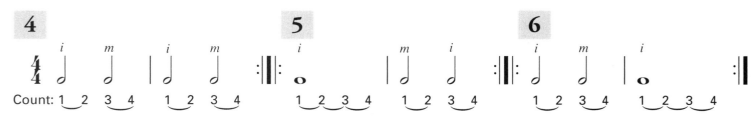

Exercise 7–9 add the quarter-note rhythm. Quarter notes receive one count. When exercises 7 and 9 are repeated, you need to begin on *m.* The idea is to always alternate the fingers.

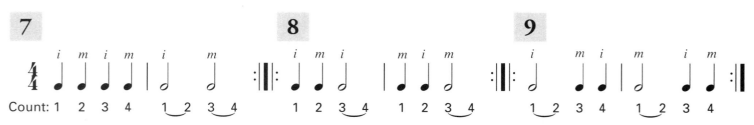

*For an explanation of repeat signs see page 71.

Rhythm Drills

The following **RHYTHM DRILLS** can be used in many different ways:
1. clap and count the rhythms
2. play the drills on various strings
3. *combine* two drills with other players
4. *combine* three drills playing the open treble strings
5. play various drills on the bass strings
6. play the drills while you practice fretting various notes
7. strum the rhythm drills on a chord or a chord progression
8. *combine* single-note playing and chord playing

Track 53 (Ex. 10–14)   Track 54 (Ex. 15–19)

Left-Hand Drill

The following exercise will develop a good left-hand technique. Repeat each note four times and **leave** the left-hand fingers on the fingerboard as they are added, and as you move from the 3rd string to the 1st string. This will force you to have a *straight wrist* and the *palm* of your hand will have to be away from the neck of the guitar.

Begin the drill on the open 3rd string. Play the open 3rd string four times and then place the first finger on the 1st fret

(play four times). Now place the second finger on the 2nd fret, 3rd string—*leaving the first finger in place*—*(play four times)*. Now add the third finger on the 3rd fret, 3rd string—*leaving both the first and second fingers in place*—*(play four times)*. Now move to the open 2nd string and continue this pattern. The point is that you need to leave the fingers on the fingerboard in order to force the hand into the proper hand position.

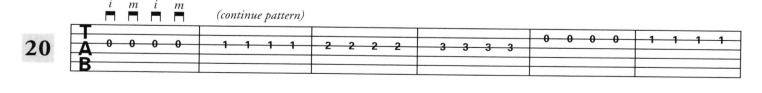

NOTES ON THE FIRST STRING

E Open, 1st string

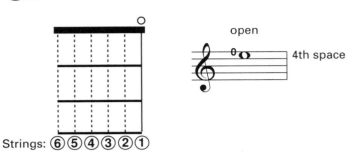

The 1st string of the guitar is the highest sounding and thinnest string. As you hold the guitar, it is the string nearest the floor. In music notation, the **OPEN E, 1ST STRING** is located on the fourth space of the staff. Open means the string is not fingered.

Exercises 21–23 introduce whole notes, half notes and quarter notes on the open E, 1st string.

PICKSTYLE

Use a *down-stroke* (◼) on each note (review page 62).

FINGERSTYLE

Alternate the index *(i)* and middle *(m)* fingers. Use a *rest stroke* (see page 63). Play the following exercises slowly. Count out loud and keep a steady beat.

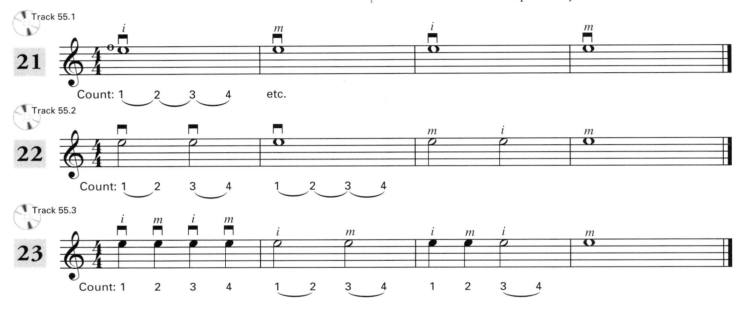

Track 55.1

21

Count: 1 2 3 4   etc.

Track 55.2

22

Count: 1 2 3 4   1 2 3 4

Track 55.3

23

Count: 1 2 3 4   1 2 3 4   1 2 3 4

F 1st fret, 1st string

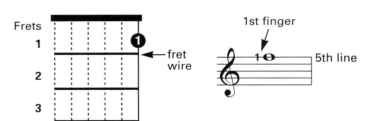

Place the first finger of the left hand on the 1st fret as close as possible to the fret wire. The fleshy part of the finger is actually touching the fret wire. Apply pressure just behind the fret wire. In music notation, the F is located on the 5th line of the music staff.

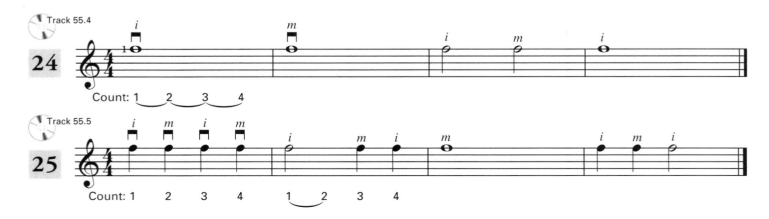

Track 55.4

24

Count: 1 2 3 4

Track 55.5

25

Count: 1 2 3 4   1 2 3 4

The E and F are now combined in the song *Mist.* You play the **SOLO** or top line. Your teacher or a friend can play the **ACCOMPANIMENT.** This song is eight measures long. When you reach the end of the 1st line continue on to the 2nd line.

Mist

*Acc. (Accompaniment) When Acc. or Solo is followed by *, it means the student will be able to play this part later.

G **3rd fret, 1st string**

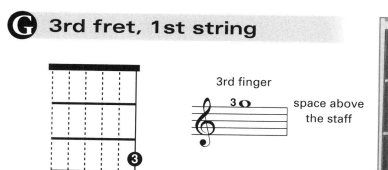

3rd finger

space above the staff

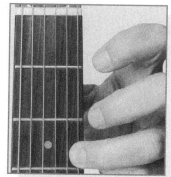

Place the third or ring finger of the left hand on the 3rd fret immediately behind the fret wire. Keep the left-hand fingers *spread apart* so that the index finger is above the 1st fret. In music notation, the G is located on the 1st space above the staff.

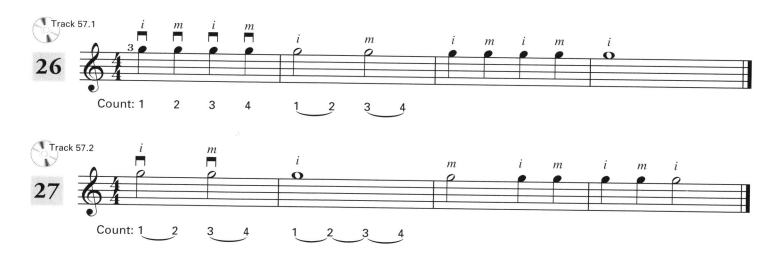

REVIEW 1st string E, F and G

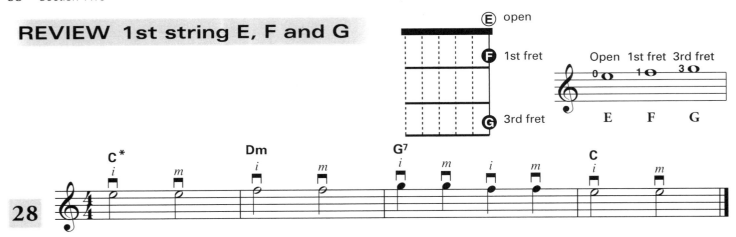

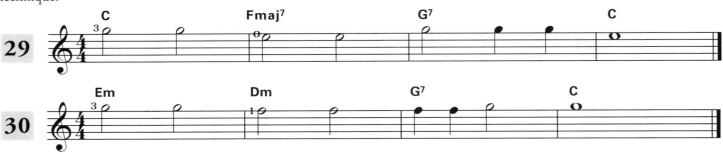

28

*In Section 2 of *Jerry Snyder's Guitar School,* chord symbols are provided so the teacher or another guitarist may accompany the student.

REVIEW Right Hand Technique

PICKSTYLE

Continue to play the notes using a down-stroke (⊓) with the pick. The down-stroke sign will be eliminated from this point unless it is needed to help clarify the right-hand technique.

FINGERSTYLE

Continue to *alternate* the index *(i)* and middle *(m)* fingers using the *rest stroke*. You can begin a song or exercise with either the index or middle finger.

29

30

Chelsie uses the 1st string E, F and G. Play the **SOLO** as your teacher or friend plays the **ACCOMPANIMENT.** Play this song at a slow tempo (speed). Keep a steady beat.

Chelsie

Track 58

J.S.

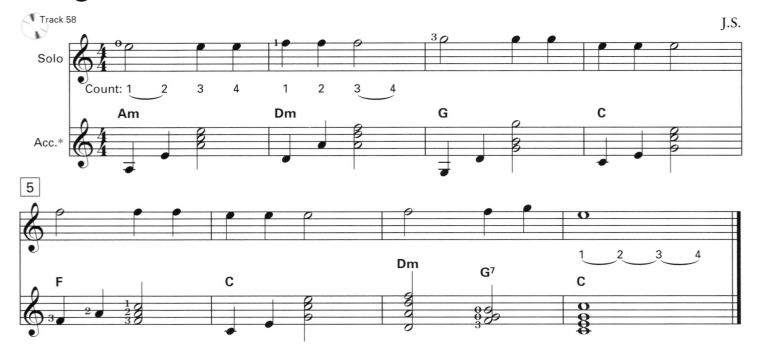

NOTES ON THE SECOND STRING

B Open, 2nd string

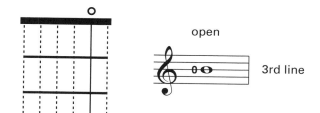

open

3rd line

The open 2nd string is tuned to B. In music notation, the B is located on the 3rd or middle line of the music staff.

Track 59.1

31

Count: 1   2   3   4   1   2   3   4

Track 59.2

32

Count: 1   2   3   4   1   2   3   4

C 1st fret, 2nd string

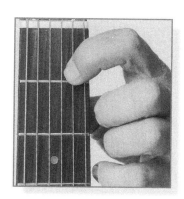

1st finger

3rd space

Place the index finger of the left hand on the 1st fret, 2nd string—just behind the metal fret. In music notation, the C is located in the 3rd space of the staff.

Track 59.3

33

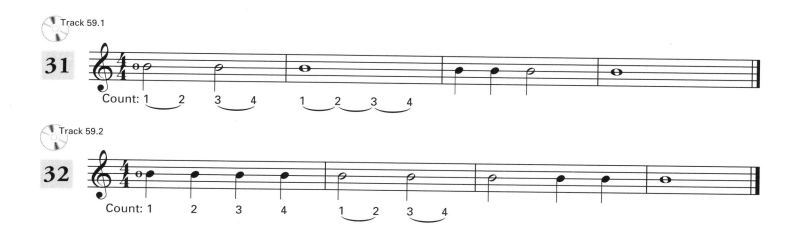

B-C *Mix*

Track 60

Solo

Acc.*

G (arpeggios)   Am   D⁷   G

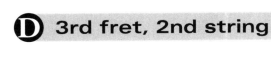 **3rd fret, 2nd string**

Place the third finger of the left hand on the 3rd fret of the 2nd string. D is located on the 4th line of the music staff.

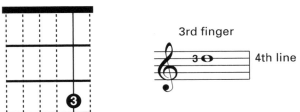

3rd finger

4th line

Track 61.1

34

Track 61.2

35

Track 61.3

36

Track 61.4

37

REVIEW Notes on the 1st and 2nd strings

Notice that the left-hand fingering pattern is the same for both the 1st and 2nd strings. Keep the fingers spread above the frets. The thumb is placed on the back of the neck at a spot that opposes the first and second fingers (see page 63).

B C D E F G

Easy Rock

Track 62

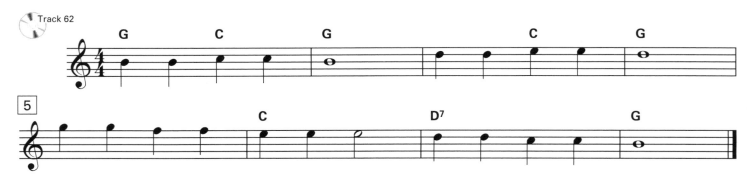

5

Tempo Markings

TEMPO refers to the *speed* of the music. Three principal tempo markings are *Andante* (slow), *Moderato* (moderately), and *Allegro* (fast).

Breezin'

Moderato

Quarter Rest

A rest is a symbol used in music to indicate *silence*. For each note, there is a corresponding rest that has the same time value. A **quarter rest** receives one count or beat. Rests are counted the same way you count notes. A parenthesis placed around the counting indicates that rests are symbols of silence.

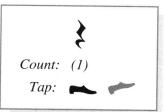

Count: *(1)*
Tap:

Count: (1)   2   3   4   (1)   2   3   4   (1)   2   3   4   1 2 3 4

Rock Out

 Track 63

Moderato
Repeat sign* D⁷

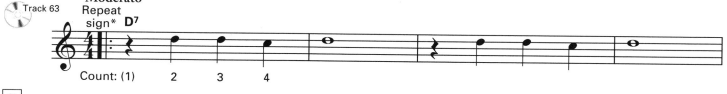

Count: (1)   2   3   4

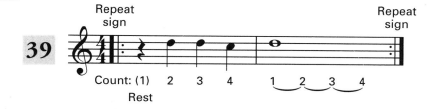
Repeat sign*

Repeat Sign

***Repeat signs** are used in music to avoid writing out repeated passages of music. The sign consists of two double bars with two dots on the inside, facing the measures to be repeated. Play the measures with the repeat signs twice.

Repeat sign   Repeat sign

39

Count: (1)   2   3   4   1   2   3   4
Rest

Dotted Half Note

A **DOT** adds one half the value to a note. A dotted half note receives three counts or beats (2 + 1). Count and tap the beats as you play.

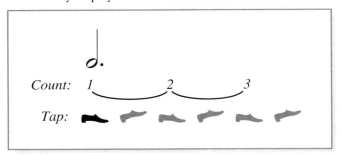

$\frac{3}{4}$ Time Signature

The $\frac{3}{4}$ **time signature** organizes the rhythm of music into three beats in each measure. The 1st beat of the measure should receive more emphasis or stress.
Count **1** 2 3 | **1** 2 3 .

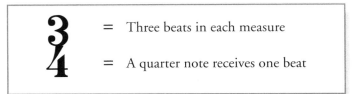

$\frac{3}{4}$ = Three beats in each measure

     = A quarter note receives one beat

Prelude

Track 64

M. Carcassi

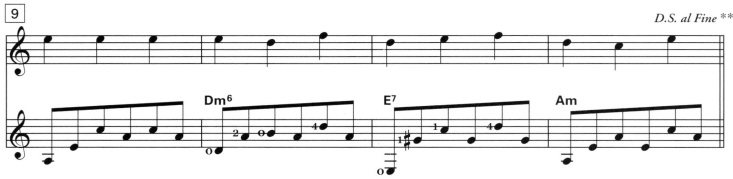

Dal Segno

Dal Segno or **D.S. means "from the sign." It is one of the signs used in music that directs the player to skip backward through the music to a place marked with a sign (𝄋).

D. S. al Fine means to go back and play from the sign to the place marked *Fine* (end). In this case, go back to the 2nd line and play it again.

Tie

A **TIE** is a curved line that connects two notes of the *same pitch*. A tie is necessary if you wish to hold a note beyond the bar line. Play the 1st note and hold it for the combined count of the two notes.

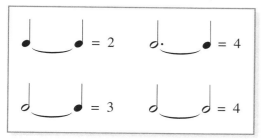

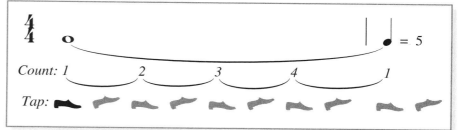

Sort of Blue

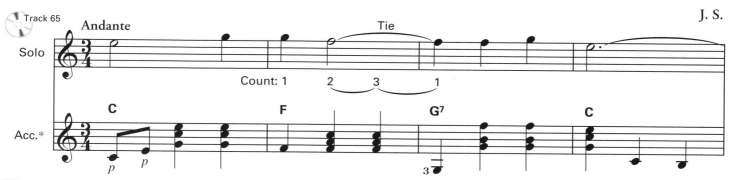

Mary Ann

NOTES ON THE THIRD STRING

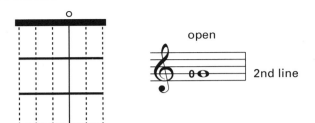 Open, 3rd string

The open 3rd string is G. It is located on the 2nd line of the music staff. When a stem is added to a quarter or half note that is written below the 3rd line of the staff, the stem is attached to the right side and extends above the note head.

40

41

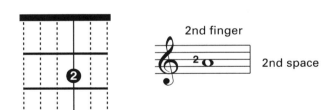 2nd fret, 3rd string

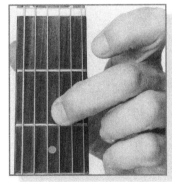

Place the second finger of the left hand on the 2nd fret, 3rd string. In music notation, the A is located on the 2nd space of the music staff.

42

43

REVIEW Notes on the 1st, 2nd and 3rd strings

44

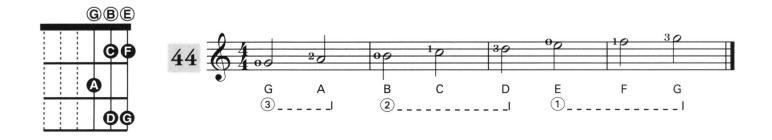

First and Second Endings

FIRST and **SECOND ENDINGS** are another way of directing the player to repeat a section of music. In *Jingle Bells,* play the 1st two lines of music and the *1st ending*. Go back to the beginning and repeat the 1st and 2nd lines of music. Skip the 1st ending and play the *2nd ending*.

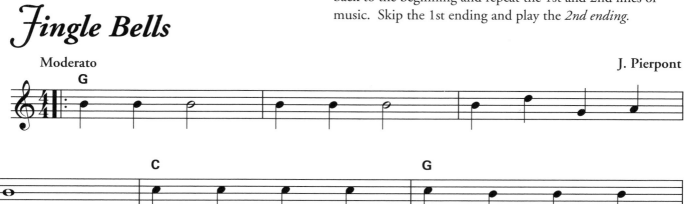

Da Capo (D.C.) al Fine

DA CAPO or **D.C.** means "from the beginning." It directs the player to go back to the beginning of the music. *D.C. al Fine* directs the player to return to the beginning of the music and to play to the place marked *Fine* (end). In *Peaceful Feeling*, play the 1st and 2nd lines of music and then repeat them (repeat sign). Now continue on and play the 3rd and 4th lines of music. Observe the *D.C. al Fine* and go back to the beginning of the music. Play the 1st and 2nd lines of music again and end at the *Fine* (the end of the 2nd line).

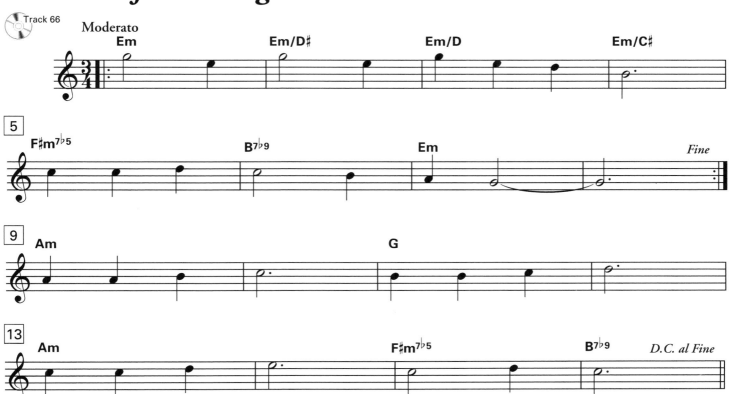

Half Step and Whole Step

The distance between two tones is called an *interval.* The smallest interval is the **HALF STEP.** Guitar frets are placed a *half step* apart on the fingerboard. In the musical alphabet—A, B, C, D, E, F, G—there are two *natural half steps.* They occur between B and C, fig. 1, and E and F, fig. 2.

Two half steps (1/2 + 1/2) equal a **WHOLE STEP.** All of the other tones in the musical alphabet are a *natural whole step* apart. For example, the interval distance between C and D, fig. 3, and F and G, fig. 4, is a *whole step.* These notes are two frets apart.

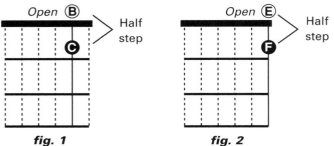

fig. 1   fig. 2

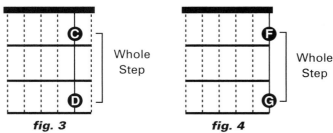

fig. 3   fig. 4

Notes located between the natural whole steps are called **SHARPS (♯)** or **FLATS (♭).** On the piano keyboard, the black keys are sharps or flats, fig. 5. On the guitar, the notes that occur between the natural whole steps are the sharps or flats.

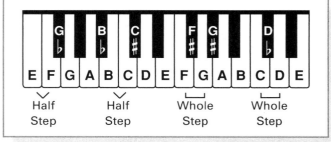

fig. 5   Piano keyboard

Sharps

When a **SHARP (♯)** is placed before a note in music notation, it *raises* the note one half step higher. On the guitar, that is the distance of one fret, fig. 6.

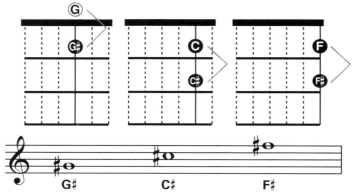

fig. 6
Sharps

G♯   C♯   F♯

♯ 2nd fret, 1st string

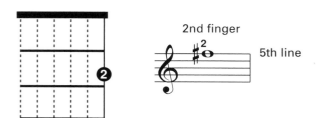

2nd finger

5th line

Place the second finger of the left hand on the 2nd fret, 1st string. The customary practice in music notation is to write the sharp once for each measure. All F's are to be played as F♯ until and up to the bar line. The bar line cancels the sharp so that it must be written in again if there are any F sharps to be played in the next measure. Play the following drill.

(Also F♯)

45

MAJOR SCALE

A scale is a series of consecutive tones moving from one tone to another. The **MAJOR SCALE** is the most commonly used scale. The major scale is a series of eight successive tones that have a pattern of whole and half steps. The major scale has a half step between the 3rd and 4th and the 7th and 8th tones of the scale. All other scale tones are a whole step apart, fig. 1.

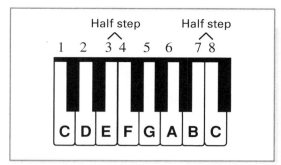

fig. 1   Keyboard analysis—C major scale

G Major Scale

In order to obtain the correct pattern of whole and half steps, an F♯ must be added to the **G MAJOR SCALE,** fig. 2 and 3.

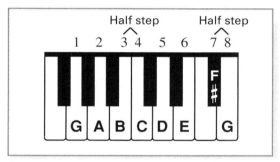

fig. 2   Keyboard analysis—G major scale

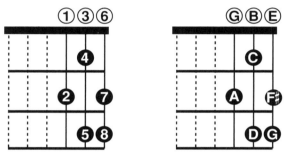

fig. 3   Fretboard analysis—G major scale

Play the G Major Scale, exercise 46. Notice the *half steps* between the 3rd and 4th and the 7th and 8th tones of the scale. Then play the *G Scale Study*.

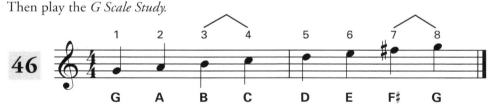

46   G A B C D E F♯ G

G Scale Study

Track 67

Key Signature

A song based on the G major scale is in the **KEY OF G MAJOR.** Since the F is sharp in the G scale, every F will be sharp in the key of G major. Instead of making all the F's sharp in the song, the sharp is indicated at the beginning, in the **KEY SIGNATURE.** Sharps or flats shown in the key signature are effective throughout the song.

Folk Song

Track 68

Key Signature:
One Sharp (F#)

French

Moderato

Principal Chords

The **principal chords** are chords built on the 1st (I), 4th (IV), and 5th (V) tones of the major scale. In the Key of G Major, the principal chords are G, C, and D^7. The G chord functions as *home base*. Most songs in the Key of G begin and end on a G chord. The D^7 is the next most frequently used chord.

G	A	B	C	D^7	E	F#	G
I			IV	V			

Principal chords in G major

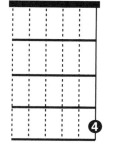 4th fret, 1st string

4th finger

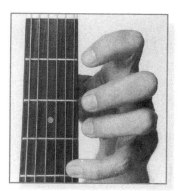

Place the fourth finger (pinky) on the 4th fret, 1st string for the G♯. Remember that the sharp only needs to be written once in each measure.

47

Natural Sign

A **natural sign** (♮) is used to *cancel* the effect of a sharp or flat. When placed before a note, it returns the note to its unaltered form.

48

Leger Lines

Leger lines are lines that are added above or below the staff to extend the range. In order to notate the A, 5th fret, 1st string, it is necessary to add one leger line above the staff.

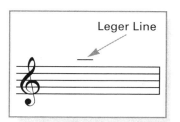
Leger Line

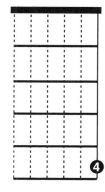 5th fret, 1st string

4th finger

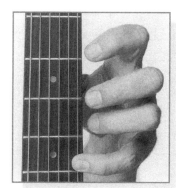

In music notation, the A, 5th fret, 1st string is located on the 1st leger line above the staff. Shift the left hand, fourth finger up to the 5th fret. You are now in *2nd position*. It is called 2nd position because the first finger is at the 2nd fret.

49

Shifting

The following exercise gives you some practice in **SHIFTING** the left hand from *1st position* to *2nd position* and back again. *Spanish Song* requires a shift to the 2nd position in order to play the A at the 5th fret.

50

Spanish Song

The tempo or speed for *Spanish Song* is indicated as *Adagio*. Adagio is a slower tempo than Andante.

Track 69   **Traditional**

**This song is played at an *Adagio* tempo so you could use all down strokes (⊓) with the pick.

OPEN BASS STRINGS

The 4th, 5th and 6th strings of the guitar are called the **BASS STRINGS.** The open 4th string is the **D** string. In music notation, it is located on the 1st space below the staff, fig. 1. The open

5th string is an A. In order to notate the A, two *leger lines* must be added below the staff. The A is located on the 2nd leger line, fig. 2. The 6th string or E string is the lowest note on

the guitar. Three leger lines need to be added to the staff to notate E. The E is located on the space below the 3rd leger line, fig. 3.

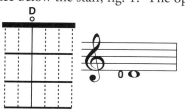

fig. 1   D—open 4th string

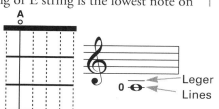

fig. 2   A—open 5th string

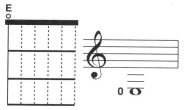

fig. 3   E—open 6th string

Use either a *down-stroke* (⊓) with a **PICK** or a *free stroke* with the **THUMB.** Review page 16 for an explanation of the free stroke. Check your arm and hand position. Be sure that your forearm is placed on the edge of the guitar just above the bridge base.

Practice both the solo and accompaniment parts in *Harvest*. The solo part begins in the 2nd position.

Harvest

Eighth Notes

An **eighth note** receives one half of a count or beat. It can be played on the *down* or on the *up* part of the beat. Eighth notes are commonly played in pairs and are attached with a beam.

fig. 1   **Eighth notes**

Eighth notes move twice as fast as quarter notes. Count them by inserting the word "an" between the numbers. For example, 1 an 2 an 3 an 4 an, fig. 2.

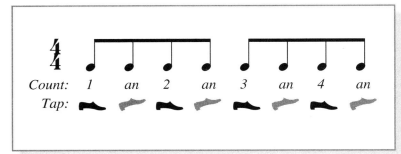

fig. 2   **Eighth notes**

Playing Techniques

PICKSTYLE

Use an **up-stroke** (V) with the pick on eighth notes that occur on the upbeat (an). In playing the *up-stroke*, the index finger pushes the pick through the string. Follow through only enough to finish picking the string and then return to the starting point. Remember to use a minimum of movement. Use **alternate** (⊓V) *down-* and *up-strokes* when you are playing a succession of eighth notes. Use the *down-stroke* (⊓) on the downbeats and the *up-stroke* (V) on the upbeats.

FINGERSTYLE

Alternate the middle and index fingers using the *rest stroke*. When crossing strings, attempt to use the index finger on the lower (sounding) string. Move to the higher (sounding) string with the middle finger. For example, if you are playing on the 3rd string, try to create an alternating pattern that allows you to move to the 2nd string with the middle finger. Conversely, if you are playing on the 2nd string, try to move to the 3rd string with the index finger.

Practice the following exercises using either the *pickstyle* or *fingerstyle* technique. Play the rhythm patterns on various open and fretted strings.

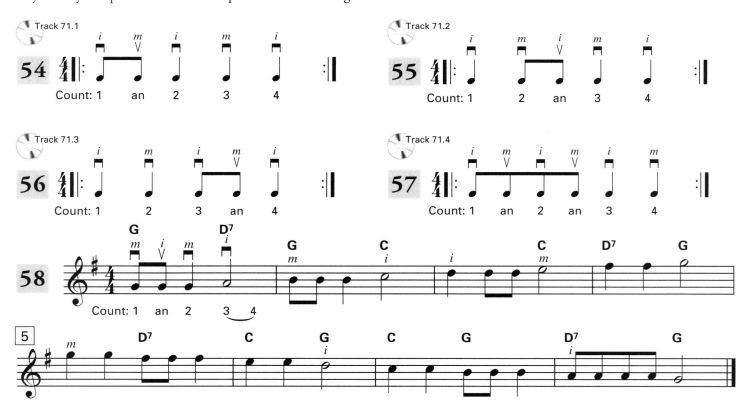

Celebrate (lead)

Ode to Joy

L. Beethoven

NOTES ON THE FOURTH STRING

E 2nd fret, 4th string

2nd finger

1st line

The **E** is located on the 4th string, 2nd fret. Use the second finger to fret the note. Play exercises 59 and 60 with a pick (⊓), the thumb (free stroke) or the fingers (*i, m*—rest strokes).

59

2

60

2   0

F 3rd fret, 4th string

3rd finger

1st space

The **F** is located on the 3rd fret, 4th string and is fingered with the third finger.

61

3

REVIEW Notes on the 4th String

The open D, 4th string was first introduced on page 81. Notice that there is only the *interval* distance of one fret between E and F. This is called a *half step* in music.

62

0

63

2

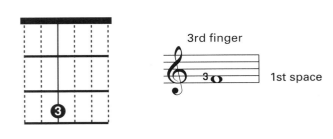

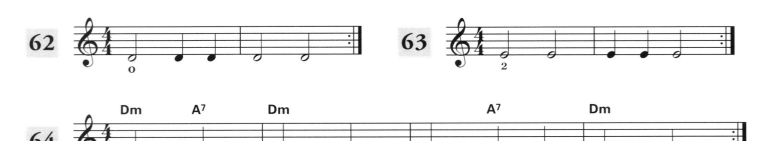

64

| Dm | A⁷ | Dm | | A⁷ | Dm |

0   2   3

The *Andantino* solo part has been created from the chords in the song—called broken chords or *arpeggios*. When playing the solo part, leave your fretted fingers down and let these notes and the open strings ring throughout the measure. Use down-strokes in pickstyle. In fingerstyle, pluck the open 3rd string with the thumb, the 2nd string with the index finger *(i)* and the 1st string with the middle *(m)* finger. *Andantino* indicates a tempo slightly faster than *andante*. Practice the solo and accompaniment to the next two songs.

Dynamics

Dynamics are signs that indicate how loudly or softly to play the music. They add interest to the music by adding contrast.

piano (p) Soft

mezzo piano (mp) Moderately Soft

mezzo forte (mf) Moderately Loud

forte (f) Loud

fortissimo (ff) Very Loud

Basic Fingerstyle Hand Position

The **Basic Fingerstyle Hand Position** requires that you *PLANT* the fingers on the **TREBLE** (3rd, 2nd and 1st) strings and the thumb on one of the **BASS** strings (6th, 5th and 4th). Using *free strokes,* chords and broken chords *(arpeggios)* can be played from this hand position.

FINGERS

Place the index *(i)* finger on the 3rd string, the middle *(m)* finger on the 2nd string and the ring *(a)* finger on the 1st string. The fingers should be stacked or bunched together, fig. 1.

THUMB

Place the thumb *(p)* on one of the bass strings. The thumb should be rigid and straight and should extend toward the guitar fingerboard so that it is not on a collision course with the fingers, fig. 2.

fig. 1   Hand position

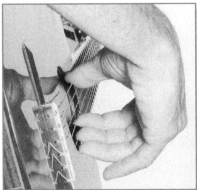

fig. 2   Hand position from underneath

Chords and Arpeggios Fingerstyle

The **Em CHORD** and **ARPEGGIO** can be played on the open strings, fig. 3 and 4. Using *free strokes,* the thumb plucks the 6th string and the fingers pluck the treble strings. It is important to *plant* the right hand before you play. The plant usually has to be done very quickly. An **arpeggio** is a

broken chord. Individual notes of the chord are plucked and allowed to *sustain* or *ring* into the next note. This produces the sound of a chord—but one note at a time. Use *free strokes* with the thumb and fingers as you play the following exercises.

Am, Dm & E Chords and Arpeggios

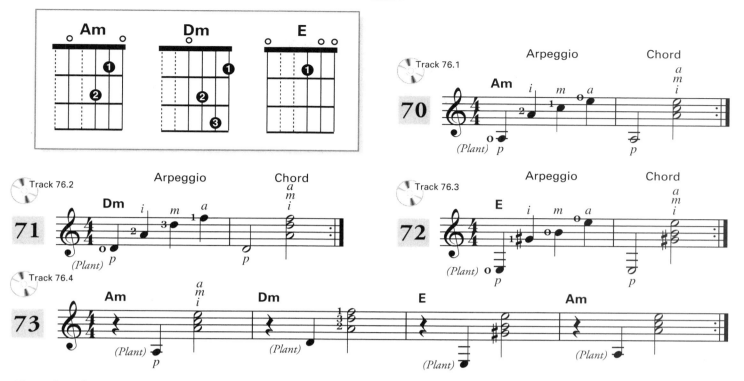

Classical Study is a combination of chords and arpeggios.

FINGERSTYLE

Use the thumb to pluck the bass strings and the fingers to pluck the treble strings. *Plant* the hand in the basic finger-style hand position at the beginning of each measure and use *free strokes*.

PICKSTYLE

Classical Study can also be played with a pick. Use down-strokes on the bass-chord patterns and alternating down-up strokes on the arpeggios.

Classical Study

Try playing the accompaniment part for the *Prelude* on page 72 and *Spanish Song* on page 80.

Flats

A **flat** (♭) placed before a note *lowers* the note one half step. If the note is *fingered*, play the next lower note or fret, fig. 1. If the note is located on an *open* string, play the 4th fret of the next lower string unless the string is the 3rd string. On the 3rd string, play the 3rd fret, fig. 2.

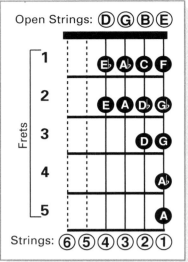

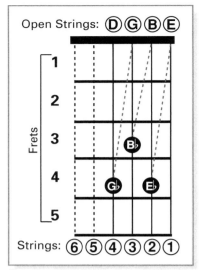

fig. 1   Flatting fingered notes   **fig. 2   Flatting open string notes**

ENHARMONICS

This is a term used to describe tones that are actually one and the same, but are *named* and *written* differently. for example, D♯ and E♭ are the same tone even though they are written differently. Study and play exercise 74. Review sharps (♯) on page 76.

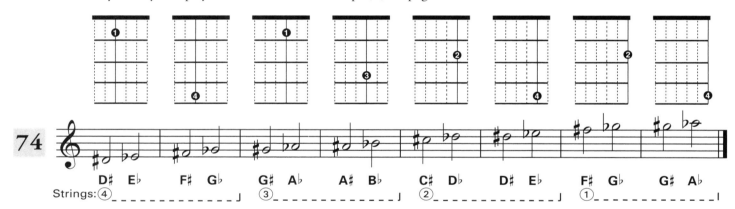

Chromatic Scale

A **chromatic scale** is a scale in which each successive note is a *half step* apart (see page 76). Exercise 75 is the **G Chromatic Scale.** It begins on the open G, 3rd string and moves by half steps up to the G, 1st string, 3rd fret. Sharps (♯) are used on the ascending chromatic scale and flats (♭) are used when the scale descends.

LEFT-HAND PLAYING TECHNIQUE

When playing the *descending scale,* it is helpful to *plant* the index finger of the left hand on the fingerboard in *preparation* for the note it will fret. For example, as you move from the 1st string to the 2nd string, place the index finger immediately on the 1st fret, 2nd string (C) as you fret the E♭ with the little finger. This promotes a good hand position, speed and accuracy. After you have played the open 2nd string (B), plant the index finger on the 1st fret, 3rd string (A♭) as you fret the B♭ with the ring finger.

Track 78

Tied Eighth Note Rhythms

As you have learned, a **TIE** is used to connect two notes of the *same pitch* (see page 73). When a tie is used with quarter, half or whole notes, it generally extends the note value across the bar line into the next measure. The tie is also used within the same measure to tie eighth notes that occur on the upbeat *(an)* to a quarter or half note. This results in rhythms that are commonly found in pop, jazz and rock music.

SYNCOPATION

In $\frac{4}{4}$ time, the normal accent (>) is on the 1st beat of the measure with the secondary accent on the 3rd beat (exercise 76). To accent a note means to stress one tone over others. When the accent is shifted to a normally weak beat, it is called *syncopation* (exercise 77). Play these two exercises on the open 1st string (E). Play the accented note a little louder.

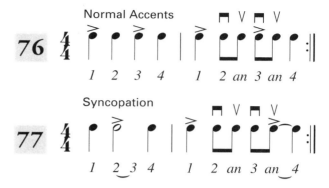

The tied eighth-note rhythms found in *Groovin'* are examples of syncopation. In preparation for playing the solo part, practice the following rhythm exercises on the open 1st string (E). Use a pick or alternate the index and middle fingers (rest strokes).

Count: (1) 2 an 3 an 4

Count: 1 an 2 an 3 4

Groovin' (lead)

Track 79

Groovin' contains two FLATS: A♭ on the 1st string in measure 4 and A♭ on the 3rd string in measure 8. You have previously played those notes as their *enharmonic* equivalent—G♯.

Groovin' (rhythm-bass)

Rock rhythms are often based on a down-stroke motion. Play the accompaniment bass line to *Groovin'* with successive down-strokes with a pick. Slightly **MUTE** the strings by allowing the heel of the right hand to rest on the strings at the bridge. This will give you a "chucking" sound. It is possible to play this part with the thumb but it is not as effective.

NOTES ON THE FIFTH STRING

The **OPEN A, 5th STRING** was introduced on page 81. **B** is located on the 2nd fret and is fingered with the second finger. **C** is located on the 3rd fret. Use the third finger to fret this note.

Practice the following exercises using either a down-stroke with a pick, free strokes with the thumb, or alternating rest strokes with the index and middle fingers.

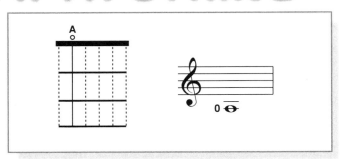

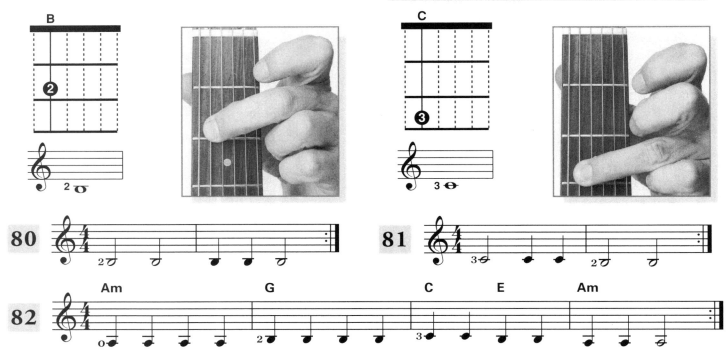

If you are using a pick, use down-strokes for each note in *Gypsy Nights*. Fingerstyle players have two options: play the notes on the bass strings with the thumb and the notes on the treble strings with the fingers, using free strokes, or play all of the notes with the index and middle fingers (alternating), using rest strokes. Notice the F♯, 4th string in measure 8.

Gypsy Nights

REVIEW Notes on the 5th, 4th and 3rd strings

Use a down-stroke with a pick or *free strokes* with the thumb *(p)*.

Dotted Quarter Note

When a **DOT** is added to a quarter note, it adds a half beat (1/2) to the value of the note. A **DOTTED QUARTER NOTE** receives one and one half beats ($1 + \frac{1}{2} = 1\frac{1}{2}$).

The dotted quarter note is most often used in a **DOTTED QUARTER-EIGHTH NOTE** rhythm pattern. This pattern exists in the beginning of two familiar songs, *London Bridge* and *Deck the Halls*.

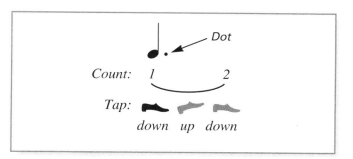

Dotted quarter note

$\frac{2}{4}$ Time Signature

The $\frac{2}{4}$ **time signature** organizes the rhythm of the music into two beats per measure. The 1st beat of the measure should receive more emphasis or stress. Count **1** 2 **1** 2.

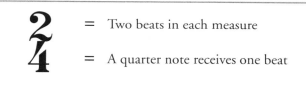

$\frac{2}{4}$ = Two beats in each measure

= A quarter note receives one beat

Play *House of the Rising Sun* using down-strokes with a pick or *free strokes* with the thumb. Fingerstyle players could also try using the alternating *rest strokes* with the index *(i)* and middle *(m)* fingers.

House of the Rising Sun

Traditional

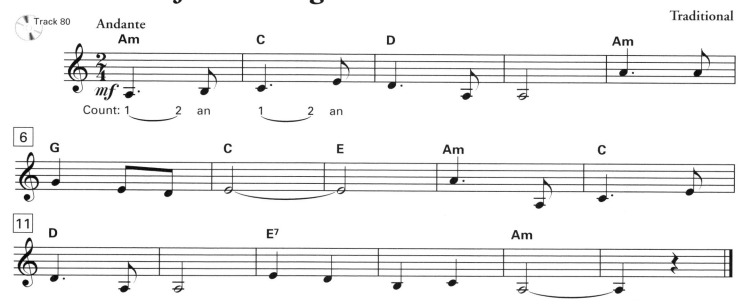

NOTES ON THE SIXTH STRING

The **OPEN E, 6th STRING** has been used in several songs and exercises since its introduction on page 81. Two additional notes on the 6th string are **F** and **G**. The F is located on the 1st fret and is fingered with the first finger. The G is located on the 3rd fret and is fingered with the third finger.

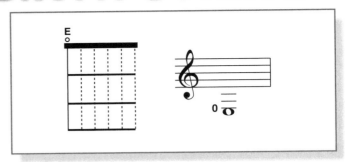

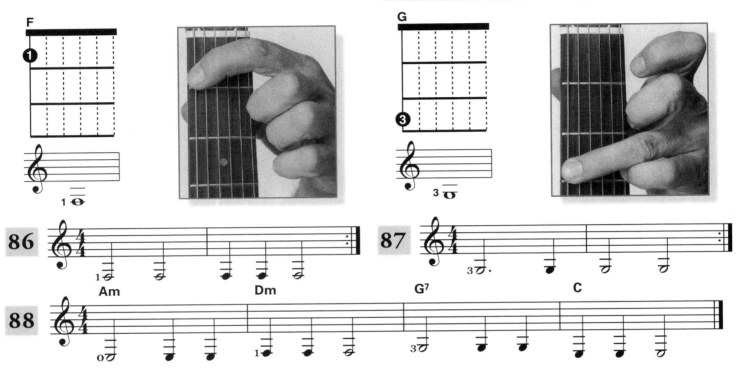

For additional practice, play the accompaniment part to *B-C Mix* on page 69, *Folk Song* on page 78, and *Ode To Joy* on page 83.

Learn both the solo and accompaniment parts to *Sleeper's Awake*. Play the accompaniment part with a pick or with free strokes with the thumb.

Sleeper's Awake (theme)

A Chromatic Scale

The **A Chromatic Scale** moves by half steps from the open A, 5th string up to the A on the 3rd string, 2nd fret. As you descend, use the *planting* technique described on page 88.

PICKSTYLE

Play the eighth notes with alternating down-up strokes with the pick.

FINGERSTYLE

Alternate the index and middle fingers on the lead. In the accompaniment, strum the chords and pluck the bass notes with the thumb.

Blues Rock

Track 82   Moderato

**FERMATA SIGN

Also known as a hold, the **fermata sign** (𝄐) tells the player to sustain a note or chord about double (but not exactly) the normal value.

Review the dotted quarter-note rhythm on page 91. Pickstyle players can use down-strokes for each note in *Scarborough Fair*. Fingerstyle players can use *free strokes* with the thumb (bass strings) and fingers (treble strings), or play all of the notes with the index and middle fingers (alternating), using rest strokes.

Scarborough Fair

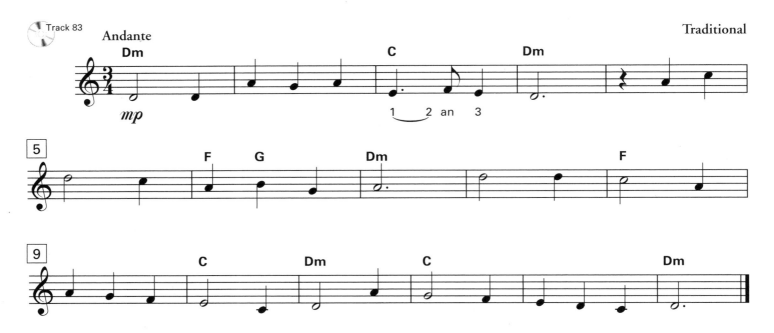

Review *House of the Rising Sun* on page 91. The following arrangement adds chords (harmony) to the melody. It is playable either in pickstyle or fingerstyle. The melody is on the bass strings except when it moves to the 3rd string in measures 5, 6 and 9. Since the song moves at a slow tempo, pickstyle players can play everything with down-strokes. Fingerstyle players should use the thumb to pluck the melody notes even when they move to the 3rd string. Pluck the chords with the fingers.

House of the Rising Sun (solo)

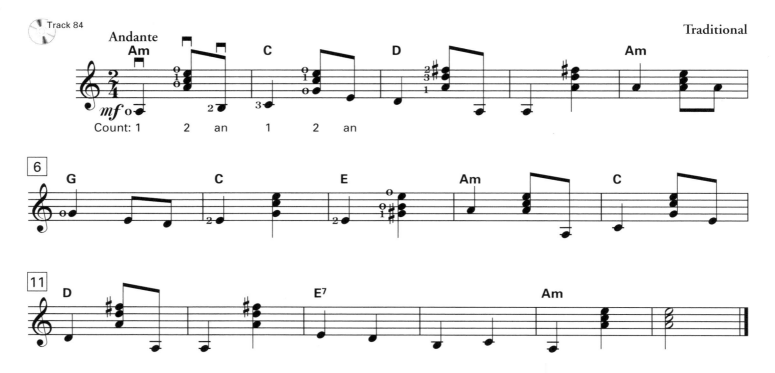

NOTE REVIEW

First Position

On the guitar, the name of the left-hand position is determined by the location of the index finger. In *1st position*, the index finger of the left hand is located at the 1st fret. Use the first finger to play the notes found on the 1st fret; that is, F on the 6th string, C on the 2nd string, and F on the 1st string. The second finger should be used to play any note located on the 2nd fret. Use the third finger for all notes located on the 3rd fret. Keep the fingers over the frets. Review page 63

for a description of a good left-hand playing position.

Play exercise 90 using downstrokes with a pick or alternating rest strokes with the index and middle fingers. Say the names of the notes as you play them. All of the notes are separated by a whole step with the exception of E to F and B to C which are half steps. The *circled numbers* placed below various notes in exercise 90 represent the strings of the guitar.

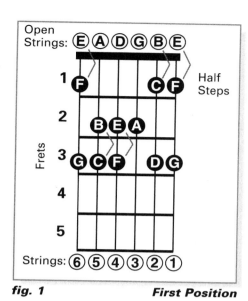

fig. 1 **First Position**

Sharps and Flats

A **SHARP** (♯) placed before a note in music notation *raises* the pitch of the note by one half step. On the guitar, that is the distance of one fret, fig. 1. A **FLAT** (♭) placed before a note in music notation *lowers* the pitch of the note by one half step, fig. 3.

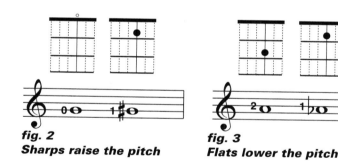

fig. 2
Sharps raise the pitch

fig. 3
Flats lower the pitch

Enharmonic Notes

The G♯ and A♭ in fig. 2 and 3 are **ENHARMONIC** notes. They represent the *same* tone but they are *named* and *written* differently. Other examples of enharmonic notes are A♯ and B♭, C♯ and D♭, F♯ and G♭. The following two diagrams are a visual representation of the sharps and flats located in first position on the guitar.

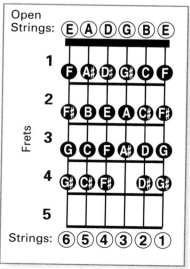

fig. 4 **Sharps**

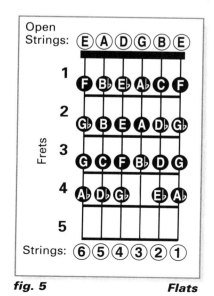

fig. 5 **Flats**

Chromatic Scale

A **chromatic scale** is a scale in which each successive note is a *half step* apart. The following exercise is a two octave **E Chromatic Scale.** This scale begins on the open 6th string and moves upward to the open 1st string. In music notation, sharps are generally used on the ascending chromatic scale. Flats are used on the descending chromatic scale.

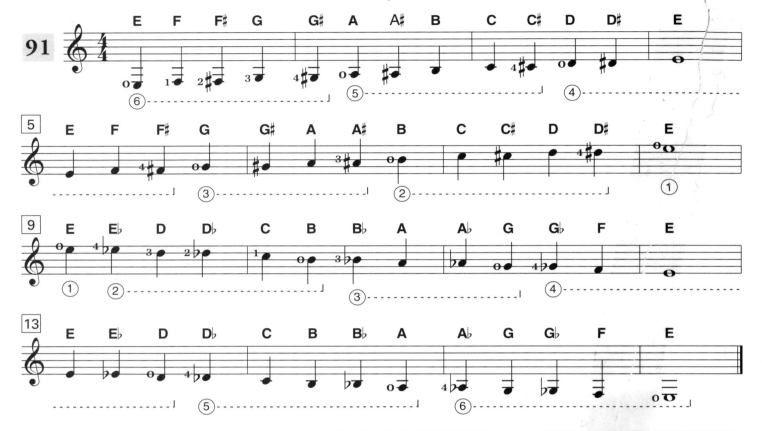

G Major Scale

The **major scale** is a series of eight successive tones that have a *specific pattern* of whole and half steps. There is always a half step between the 3rd and 4th tones and the 7th and 8th tones of the scale, fig. 1. The interval distance between the first note of the scale and the eighth note is called an **OCTAVE** . The following *G Scale Study* is a two-octave exercise. Notice the **F♯** (F sharp) on the 4th and 1st strings.

Use your fourth finger on the 4th string. When using the fourth finger, your hand must be balanced (see page 63, fig. 5). It is important for the fourth finger to be comfortable and not to have to stretch and reach for the 4th fret. Favor the position of the fourth finger. It is shorter and cannot stretch and reach sideways as easily as the first finger. Use either pickstyle or fingerstyle right-hand playing techniques.

fig. 1   **G major scale analysis**

1	2	3	4	5	6	7	8
G	A	B	C	D	E	F♯	G

Key Signature (Play all F's as F♯)

fig. 2   **Two octave G scale**

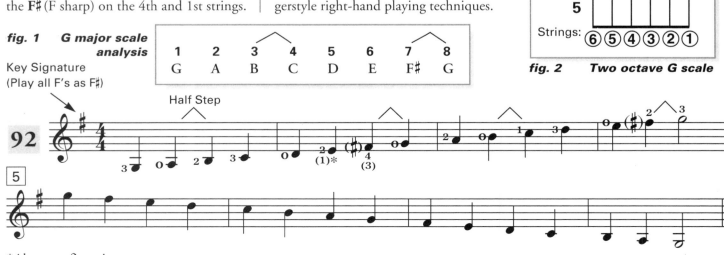

*Alternate fingering.